HARGREAVES
new illustrated
BESTIARY

HARGREAVES
new illustrated
BESTIARY

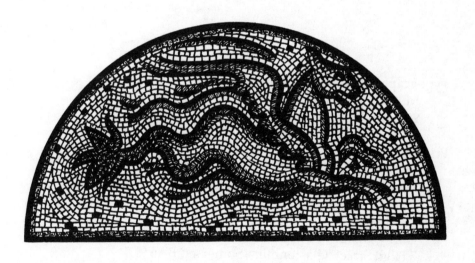

JOYCE HARGREAVES

GOTHIC IMAGE
PUBLICATIONS

HARGREAVES
new illustrated
BESTIARY

First published in Great Britain by Gothic Image Publications

© Joyce Hargrcaves 1990

Typographic design and typesetting:
    Michael Mepham
    22 Bath Road, Frome, Somerset, BA11 2HH

Printed by:
    The Guernsey Press
    PO Box 57, Braye Road, Vale, Guernsey, Channel Islands

Published by:
    Gothic Image Publications
    7 High Street, Glastonbury, Somerset, BA6 9DP

British Library CIP data
    HARGREAVES, Joyce
    HARGREAVES NEW ILLUSTRATED BESTIARY
    1. Fabulous Beasts
    i. Title
    398 . 469

ISBN 0-906362-12-1

Introduction

There are three ways in which it is possible to trace the history of Fabulous Beasts; by oral tradition, by artistic representation and by the written word. Common beliefs take form whenever people begin to share life together and it was in the ancient Near East that the earliest communities of any size were formed. Some of the earliest depictions of Fabulous Beasts come from clay tablets found in this area. In Mesopotamia the human-headed bird Zû was a protagonist in one myth found on some of these tablets and others from Ninevah portrayed a creation myth – the Enuma Elish – that featured one of the best known fabulous creatures, the dragoness Tiãmat and her death at the hands of the God Marduk.

Other major written sources are found in the works of Herodotus, Ctesias and others from the fifth to the third centuries BC, and in 'The Natural History of Pliny' written by Gaius Plinius Secundus (Pliny the Elder) in the first century AD. All of these works influenced an anonymous author, now known as the Physiologus, who wrote a serious book about natural history upon which most of the medieval bestiaries were founded. Although many of the creatures included in his work and in the bestiaries exist, there were also those that were fabulous, known only through hearsay and mythology.

The word myth, nowadays, is considered to be a pejorative word that implies false-hood, but mythology in its original sense meant a reflection of reality, truth in an irrational form palatable because of its disguise. S. H. Hooke said in his book 'Middle Eastern Mythology' that "The myth is a product of human imagination arising out of a definite situation and is intended to do something. Hence the right question to ask about a myth is not, 'is it true?' but 'what is it intended to do?' " He considers that myths, like the one featuring Tiãmat were part of a ritual which consisted of a portion that was 'done' – the dromenon – and the spoken part called in Greek the mythos or myth where the 'words of power' were an essential part of the ritual. When the Enuma Elish was enacted and chanted, the repetition of the magical words had the power to bring about a change in the situation for "The function of the myth was not knowledge but action, action essential for the very existence of the community; as an essential part of the ritual it helped to secure those conditions upon which the life of the community depended." In early civilizations, from about 3400 BC onwards, when fertility myths were enacted, at some point in the dromenon, there would sometimes be a human sacrifice. J. G. Frazer wrote of a voluntary victim, the meriah, of the Khonds of India. He was consecrated and identified with the divinity to be sacrificed and the people prayed to the Goddess of the Earth, "O Goddess, we offer thee this sacrifice; give us good harvests, good seasons and good health." The meriah was then mercifully drugged with opium and, after he had been strangled, they cut him into pieces. Each of the villages received a fragment of his body which they buried in the fields. The remainder was burnt and the ashes spread over the land. This grim sacrifice corresponds to the myth of the dismemberment of a primordial deity like Tiãmat or the Hittite serpent/dragon Illuyankas.

It is generally agreed that Fabulous Beasts are products of the imagination. But it would be worthwhile to look more closely at the definition of the word 'imagination' as, like the term 'myth', it has become a debased and almost accusatory word. Imagination is the mental faculty of forming images or concepts of external objects not present to the senses; it is closely linked to the subjective state of fantasy – the faculty of inventing images. Everyone has imagination; it is a basic element in our makeup. But what purpose does imagination serve? Why are such things as Fabulous Beasts created?

Imagination is a constructive effort to investigate the workings of instinct, intuition and states of being, to explore the ever expanding realm of possibilities that cannot be seen but only imagined and put into visual form by artistic representation. This, in turn, will lead to an emotional or some other bodily response on the part of the viewer whose behaviour can be influenced by these images. When particular attributes such as power, strength, and fearsomeness are needed to motivate an army, what better symbol could be adopted than the combination of a savage animal, an eagle and a snake – a dragon!

The conscious putting together of parts of different animals, in this way, enables the feelings that the image engenders to be expressed more fully than was previously possible. In preliterate societies and even today, as can be seen on television, visual imagery is used to carry coded information: people consciously or unconsciously transform objects or forms into symbols which constitute an international language transcending the normal limits of communication. This language is a code that must be broken to be understood for it makes possible the perception of fundamental relationships between seemingly diverse forms or appearances.

When Fabulous Beasts are created, forms found in nature are interchanged in part or completely, mixed or set apart, expanded or contracted, coarsened or polished to become creatures whose antecedents are not in doubt but whose final shapes must be considered to be imaginary. It is almost impossible to classify any one beast accurately and, with such a wealth of subject matter, it is difficult to decide which beasts to include within the confines of a book of this size; so I have adopted the following criteria.

Only creatures that already have a history be it from antiquity, classical, or from mythology will be included; modern examples will have to await the test of time. Gods with animal appendages, such as the animal-headed Egyptian Gods, do not have a place here as it is generally considered that the animal heads were representations used to support and clarify essential functions of nature and are thus an aspect of the God. Completely human creatures like giants, gnomes and Sciapods (Foot-shade Men) are excluded as are fabulous beasts that are found only in heraldry, for heraldic beasts have completely different terms of reference. There are five different types of Fabulous Beast to be found in this book: animal combinations, consisting of a beast composed of the different parts of two, three or more animals – the Griffin and the Mermecoleon; animal/human combinations – the Centaur and the Sphinx; beasts that have an excess or deficiency of parts of the body – the Hydra and the Three-legged Ass; creatures who have a natural biological shape but whose characteristics are abnormal – the Pelican in her Piety and the Halcyon, and beasts that can metamorphose into humans or other animals and vice versa.

As the distribution of these creatures is worldwide, most are known by a variety of names. So, if the bird or animal that you are seeking does not appear in the alphabetically arranged text, look for it in the index of alternative names that will be found at the back of the book. The illustrations come from a rich variety of sources being drawings of sculptures, bas reliefs, metalwork and copies of artwork found in bestiaries. Other fruitful starting points include the living masks of the North West American Indian Cannibal Birds, tomb paintings and papyri, and the written descriptions of fabulous creatures found in traveller's tales like 'The Tales of Sir John Mandeville' – a fabulous person, who was himself a literary invention. Where I have not found a suitable subject to illustrate, I have taken the liberty of inventing it myself using the written description as a guide.

The Bestiary

An Achlis leaning against a tree.

ACHLIS

The Achlis was one of the beasts described by Gaius Plinius Secundus (Pliny the Elder) in his book "The Natural History of Pliny" written in the first century AD. This extraordinary herbivore was related in shape and size to the Elk and had an enormous upper lip which was so large that the animal had to graze by moving backwards through its pasture, otherwise its lip would double back upon itself. The Achlis could never lie down as it lacked joints in its hind legs; in order to sleep, it had to recline against a tree. It was far too fleet of foot to be captured in any ordinary fashion and the only way to trap it, was to cut nearly through the tree trunk where the creature usually rested. When it leaned against the trunk, both tree and Achlis would fall down. The beast would then be unable to get to its feet as its stiff legs prevented it from rising and so could easily be caught.

AHUIZOTL

The Ahuizotl (Ah-wit-zotl), whose name means Water Opossum, was one of Mexico's magical creatures. It was as big as a dog, with monkey's paws and an extra hand on the end of its tail. This strange predator would entice a compassionate human being to it by sitting near the river crying like a child. However, its intentions were evil, for the Ahuizotl would seize the unsuspecting person with the hand on the end of its long flexible tail and drown him in the river.

When the corpse reappeared after about three days, its eyes, teeth and nails were missing. These parts of the body had been eaten by the Ahuizotl who considered them to be a delicacy. When the Mexican people found a body in this condition it was believed that the person's spirit had been called to Heaven by the rain gods.

AITVARAS

See also Serpent

The Aitvaras is a serpent that has the head of a Zaltys and a long tail which emits fire and sparks as it flies across the sky. Sometimes the Aitvaras assumes the form of a golden cockerel. The Zaltys, which the Aitvaras resembles, were grass snakes which were often kept as house pets by Lithuanians and Latvians. They were so beloved by the Goddess Saule, that she wept whenever one died. The harmless aspects of the Zaltys indicate that the Aitvaras is a creature of good omen and anyone who is fortunate enough to see one may be sure of obtaining wealth. Less fortunately, an infestation of these creatures can damage crops. Like Mari (a spirit in Basque folklore, who can appear as a serpent, a woman with bird's feet or a fireball), the Aitvaras seems to have connections with meteors and fireballs. Mari can also travel through the air emitting flames and trailing sparks and like Aitvaras can bring gifts or ruin crops.

AL BORAK

In Islam, the story is told of the Night Journey taken by the Prophet Mohammed. He rode upon the Archangel Gabriel's silver or milk white steed whose name, Al Borak, means shining or lightning; she is also known as Buraq or Burak. Al Borak is considered to be a symbol of divine love and is said to have great pureness of heart. In miniatures of her, Al Borak is generally portrayed galloping from right to left across the picture – from knowledge towards love.

Paintings of this miraculous creature give her the body of a horse, the ears of an ass, peacock plumage, the face of a woman, and she was often winged. In a book on the life of Mohammed, written by a long-forgotten author, the mare Al Borak is described as having a long mane entwined with fine pearls, daisies and hyacinths; her ears were embellished with emeralds; her right temple was sprinkled with set pearls and her left with golden flecks. Her chest and back were studded with precious stones and her eagle-like wings were also set with pearls. She exhaled the odours of musk and saffron and, although she could not speak, she could hear and understand everything that was said to her.

On the Night Journey, Al Borak first descended to Hell with Mohammed and then ascended with him to Jerusalem, and thence to the seven planetary spheres that make up the Heavenly World. Mohammed spoke in each of the Heavens with the patriarchs and angels that he found there, before

An Aitvaras

Al Borak returned the prophet to Earth. As each of the strides of Al Borak equalled the furthest range of human vision, Mohammed travelled so quickly that he was able on his return to catch a pitcher which he had upset as he left.

The steed Al Borak with Mohammed, based on a 14th century miniature from Istanbul.

AMMUT

The Egyptian 'Book of the Dead' describes the journey that the soul of a deceased person has to make in the underworld and how it is eventually brought before the God Osiris in the Hall of Judgement. The heart of the dead person is weighed against the feather of truth, on a pair of scales, by the jackal-headed God Anubis and the result is recorded by Thoth, the ibis-headed scribe and god of wisdom. The soul swears not to have caused hunger, grief or death, nor to have stolen food meant for the dead, never to have used false weights, taken babies' milk, driven livestock from their pasture or captured the birds of the Gods. If the soul is pure and has committed none of these sins, the heart is light and weighs less than the feather. The pure soul is then released into eternal bliss. If the heart is heavier than the feather, a different fate awaits the soul for, sitting at the feet of Anubis, is the monster Ammut who is also known as Am-mit, Bone-eater, Devourer and Corpse-eater. She is portrayed in various ways but the most usual interpretation of this beast gives her the head of a crocodile, the torso of a lion and the hindquarters of either a lion or a hippopotamus. The names 'Bone-eater' and 'Devourer' describe her duties for if the heart weighs heavy with sin, the soul is seized and devoured by Ammut and the spirit of the dead person ceases to exist.

Ammut, the Bone-eater. From the 'Papyrus of Ani'.

Detail of embroidery from the Syon cope. St. Michael fighting an Amphisbaena.

AMPHISBAENA

See also Dragon

The Amphisbaena is a dragon or serpent with an extra head at the end of its tail which is capable of giving a venomous bite with both sets of fangs; it is sometimes depicted with the claws of a bird and the pointed wings of a bat. There are two reasons why it is not easy to kill the Amphisbaena. It can move with great speed over the ground both forwards and backwards (the name Amphisbaena in Greek means "goes both ways" and, if it should ever be cut in half, the two parts are capable of joining together again. John Greenleaf Whittier wrote of it in 1893 in a poem 'The Double-headed Snake of Newbury' :-

"For he carried a head where his tail should be,
And the two of course could never agree,
But wriggled about with main and might,
Now to the left and now to the right;
Pulling and twisting this way and that,
Neither knew what the other was at."

Alchemical Amphisbaena symbolizing Mercury.

According to Pliny the Elder, it gives protection in pregnancy when alive, a cure for rheumatism when dead. Paul Diel, describing the symbolism associated with this creature, stated that it was probably a figure intended to express the horror and anguish associated with ambivalent situations. In Christian symbolism it is the negative side of the Amphisbaena which receives emphasis as it appears as the 'Adversary' – a concept which later became attached to the devil – which must be fought and mastered by heroes and saints.

In alchemy the amphisbaena is the symbol of the metal Mercury (Quicksilver) which is supposed to transform the base metal of the earth into gold and silver. However, the dual nature of the two-headed beast equally well describes the positive and negative forces of the earth as symbolized by the caduceus. The two heads also represent the dual nature of mercury which is both metal and liquid.

APOCALYPTIC BEASTS

See also Dragon, Hydra

A Wyvern that is also an Amphisbaena. From a 12th century bestiary.

The Apocalypse (The Revelations of St. John) is a book of the Bible rich in animal symbolism in the shape of fabulous beasts. This is probably because the apocalyptic writers often used animal aberrations to convey the presence of evil. St. John described his writings as prophesy but the exact nature of this prophesy and the meaning of these strange beasts are open to many different interpretations.

The Beast that rises out of the Sea is one of the evil creatures associated with the dragon.

12

*"And I stood upon the sand of the sea, and saw a beast
rise up out of the sea, having seven heads and ten
horns and upon his horns ten crowns and upon his
heads the name of blasphemy.*

*And the beast which I saw was like unto a leopard, and
his feet were as the feet of a bear, and his mouth as
the mouth of a lion: and the dragon gave him his
power, and his seat, and great authority.*

*And I saw one of his heads as it were wounded unto
death; and his deadly wound was healed."*

The Beast that comes out of the Earth is a companion beast
to the sea creature but is quite different in imagery. He had
two horns like a lamb and spoke as a dragon.

*"And he exerciseth all the power of the first beast before
him, and causeth the earth and them which dwell
therein to worship the first beast whose deadly
wound was healed ... saying to them that dwell on
earth that they should make an image to the beast
which had the wound by the sword and did live.*

*And he had the power to give life unto the image of the
beast, that the image of the beast should both speak,
and cause that as many as would not worship the
image of the beast should be killed.*

*And he causeth all, both small and great, rich and poor,
free and bond, to receive a mark in their right hand,
or in their foreheads: And that no man might buy or
sell, save that he had the mark, or 'the name of the
beast', or the number of his name.*

*Here is wisdom. Let him that hath understanding count
the number of the beast: for it is the number of a
man; and his number is six hundred threescore and
six."*

The Scarlet Beast is the mount of the Whore of Babylon
who, dressed in scarlet and purple and covered with gold,
precious stones and pearls, sits on her back. This scarlet
coloured beast is hydra-headed having seven heads and ten
horns. Together the pair represent decadence.

The Four Beasts are sometimes said to represent the
cardinal virtues and are also the symbols of the four evan-
gelists:

*"... and round about the throne, were four beasts full of
eyes before and behind. And the first beast was like a
lion, and the second beast like a calf, and the third
beast had the face of a man, and the fourth beast was
like a flying eagle. And the four beasts had each of
them six wings about him, and they were full of eyes
within."*

**"The Beast from the Sea."
From Master Bertram's
Workshop in Hamburg,
Germany. 1400** AD.

Opposite

"The Scarlet Beast." From a
14th century tapestry made
in Angers, France.

14

Drawing of a 12th century
Aspidochelone.

ASPIDOCHELONE

The Aspidochelone or Asp Turtle, also known as Fastito-
calon and in the East as Zaratan, is to be found in a morali-
sing bestiary called The Physiologus, the title of which
means 'one versed in natural history'. The Physiologus is
reputed to have been written in Alexandria in the second
century BC. Bestiaries derived from this book were extremely popular in the middle ages; many of them had a religious
theme and, by means of moral tales, preach warnings
against drunkenness and other vices.

In the earlier bestiaries, the Aspidochelone (the Asp
Turtle) was not, as its name suggests, a type of turtle but a
great sea monster with a thick stone-like skin. When it
basked lazily on the surface of the water, it resembled a

rocky, moss-covered island and fooled sailors into thinking it to be actual land. However, the sailors were in for a shock when they moored their ships to this false island, for when they kindled a fire on its back to cook their food, the heat caused the Asp Turtle to dive to the bottom of the sea taking both ship and sailors with it. In later bestiaries the rock-like shape of the Aspidochelone was changed to the more familiar form of a gigantic whale.

A creature from a book of Sea Monsters.

This whale was said to be the creature that swallowed Jonah when he was thrown into the sea and its open mouth, like that of the Dragon, symbolized Hell. Here the sinking of Jonah into the darkness of the watery abyss inside the great fish symbolized the unconsciousness of death followed by resurrection.

One bestiary describes the habits of this sea creature in a moral tale where the whale represents the Devil and the sweet smell that issues from its mouth signifies the seductive snares of the tempter. Here the whale:-

'Lusts after food
then oceanward
his mouth opens
his wide lips,
a pleasant odour
comes from his inside,
so that thereby other
kinds of sea fishes
are deceived;
eager they swim to
where the sweet odour
cometh out;
they there enter
in heedless shoal,
'til the wide jaw
is filled;
then suddenly
around their prey
together crash
the grim gums.'

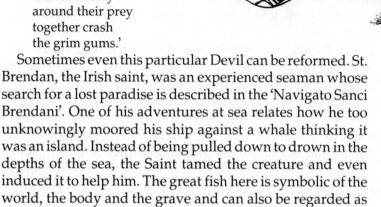

Sometimes even this particular Devil can be reformed. St. Brendan, the Irish saint, was an experienced seaman whose search for a lost paradise is described in the 'Navigato Sanci Brendani'. One of his adventures at sea relates how he too unknowingly moored his ship against a whale thinking it was an island. Instead of being pulled down to drown in the depths of the sea, the Saint tamed the creature and even induced it to help him. The great fish here is symbolic of the world, the body and the grave and can also be regarded as a symbol of containing and concealing.

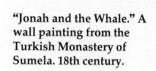

"Jonah and the Whale." A wall painting from the Turkish Monastery of Sumela. 18th century.

ASS

The Roxburgh Bestiary states that the little Ass (Asellus) was so named from being sat upon – from the word seat or saddle (a sede). The author of this book wrote that the Ass was a symbol of the Devil, for he brays about the place night and day, hour by hour, seeking his prey.

C. G. Jung in 'Symbols of Transformation' also described the Ass as an attribute of Satan in his capacity as the 'Second Sun'; it is always on heat and hated by Isis. It has been regarded as a messenger of death – the destroyer of a lifespan – although, in medieval times, it often symbolized the virtues of humility, patience and courage. In alchemy the Ass was depicted as a three-headed monster defined as a daemon triunus, a chthonian trinity. Each head represented one of the three material principles of matter – salt, sulphur and mercury.

The Ass with three legs can be found in Zoroastrian mythology. The Bundahish, a supplement of the prophet Zarathustra's written work, contains a description of the Three Legged Ass. It stands in the middle of the ocean, its coat is white, its food is spiritual and it is full of righteousness. The ocean is purified by its piss and its dung is amber. This Ass is a truly gigantic creature for each of its three hooves occupies the space that would be taken by a thousand sheep. It has six eyes, two in their rightful place, two on the crown of its head and two in its forehead which enable the Ass to see everything clearly and sharply. It has nine mouths, three can be seen in its face, three in its forehead and three on the inside of its loins. Each of these mouths is the size of a cottage. Its single horn is hollow and made of gold and from it sprout out a thousand branchlets which makes this horn a terrible weapon. Only the wicked should fear this creature for, with its keen eyesight and its powerful horn, it will conquer evil and destroy the enemies of virtue.

The Papstesel was said to be found during a flood that occurred in Italy in the fifteenth century. It had the head of an ass on a woman's body, one of its legs was that of an eagle, the other was shaped like the leg of an ox. One arm was an elephant's trunk, its tail was a serpent and it had the head of a bearded man on its back. Illustrations of this nauseating creature were used as a symbol of the Papacy's corruption during the sixteenth century. It was known as the Papstesel or Pope Ass.

Pope-ass. A drawing based on a woodcut by Lukas Cranach. 1496.

A Ba carrying a Shen, symbolic of eternity.

BA

See also Human-headed Birds.

The ancient Egyptians considered that a being was made up of several 'vehicles', of which the most commonly known are the Ba, the Ka and the Khat. The Ba was the soul, the Ka was the 'double', an abstract personality resident in the body (or the tomb) and the Khat was the physical body.

In Egyptian tomb paintings and papyri the Ba was externalised as a human headed bird of either sex. Often it was depicted with human arms added to its bird-like body. The Ba was portrayed in this form because birds are often symbols of the spirit and of the ability to enter a higher state of consciousness. The human head denotes a seat of life force and wisdom. When the head and the bird are combined, the resulting creature represents supernatural wisdom and the power of the soul to leave the body at will. In pictorial imagery, upon the death of the Khat, the Ba leaves the body in the shape of a bird, the soul bird.

BARNACLE GOOSE

The myth that the Barnacle Goose hatched from the inside of a common ship's barnacle originated in the twelfth century AD. It was at this period that Giraldus Cambrensis wrote a book 'Topographia Hiberniae' which described his travels in Ireland and an account of the life history of Barnacle Geese.

He said that there were many small birds on the west coast of Ireland called Bernacae. They were sea birds smaller than marsh geese; they did not mate, build a nest or hatch eggs for their birth was extraordinary. The birds were engendered from fir timber that had been tossed about in sea water. The first sign that a goose was about to be born was a sticky patch of a gum-like substance on the surface of the wood. The sticky knob hardened on the outside and formed a shell covering the body of the bird which was attached to the timber by its beak. Sometimes there could be as many as a thousand of these

Previous page
'The Goddess of the Sycamore Tree Welcoming the Deceased'. Wall painting 16th – 14th century BC.

A Barnacle Goose based on a drawing from Ray Lankester's 'Diversions of a Naturalist'.

small creatures hanging down from a piece of timber on the sea shore, already formed inside their shells. Soon their bodies would become covered with feathers and, when strong enough, they would discard the barnacle shell and fly away or fall into the water. A goose who fell onto land would not survive.

Not long after Cambrensis's account of the Barnacle Goose was published, there appeared, in an encyclopedia by Vincent of Beauvais, another description of the habitat of the geese. The author related how the birds were created from barnacles that grew on actual trees rooted on the sea shore. These accounts and others similar to them were so widely believed that the Barnacle Goose (an actual bird, only the account of its birth is fabulous) was eaten in Lent as it was claimed to be fish and not flesh. Although the Barnacle Goose was first described in the manuscript of Giraldus Cambrensis, there are pictures of fledglings similar to it on pottery dated from before 800 BC. These pots from Crete, Mycenae and Troy also show the unusual stalk and the rudimentary duct of the barnacle. There are a number of different names for these birds including Bernicles, Barhatas, Clacuse and Clarkgeese.

BASILISK

See also Cockatrice

The Basilisk is acknowledged to be the king of the snakes, the absolute monarch of smaller reptiles and although it is less than one metre long, it is said to be as savage as the most destructive of Dragons. Pliny the Elder, in the 1st century AD described the Basilisk as a serpent which carried itself proudly erect and was so poisonous that if a man pierced it with a spear, the poison ran straight up the metal of the weapon and into his arm like an electric current.

At first, pictures of the Basilisk showed a serpent with a narrow pointed head topped by three excrescences which stood up on it like a crest, but later the creature acquired a shape more in keeping with its regal and horrific reputation. It was portrayed with a thicker and heavier body than its previous serpentine one; a body that was supported by bird-like legs. A particularly savage Basilisk from Saxony was described as very fat with a speckled white body, blue back and a coiled tail.

Most Basilisks are illustrated in bestiaries and early natural history books with the crest on the top of their heads actually in the form of a crown. This crown is a reminder that the Basilisk is a royal creature and is the reason why sometimes it has been regarded as identical with the Uraeus serpent of Egypt, symbol of divine rulership. The name Basilisk comes from the word basileus which means king and basilica, a royal palace, is derived from the same source.

The Basilisk lived in the desert; in fact it was the cause of the desert, for the breath of this venomous beast was so destructive that it could wither all the surrounding vegetation and even set fire to stones. The smell of its sweat would destroy any living being and the waters of the streams where it quenched its thirst became so poisonous that they remained lethal for centuries. This creature could also spit out its venom into the air and any bird flying past would be instantly annihilated by the monster's poison.

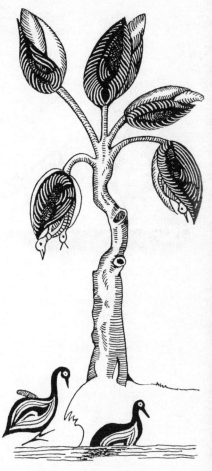

Barnacle Goose Tree.

But the most potent weapon in the Basilisk's armoury was not its poison but its glowing eyes; one searing glance from its eyes was enough to kill a man instantly, hence the expression, still in use today, that describes a riveting glare as a "basilisk stare". This murderous stare was, fortunately for its prospective victim, also its own downfall for the sight of its own reflected stare in a mirror was enough to kill the Basilisk itself.

Two creatures were capable of killing the Basilisk. The weasel could kill it by biting it to death and the crowing of a cock sent it into a fit from which it never recovered. During the first century AD the deserts of North Africa were said to be infested with these serpentine creatures and travellers crossing the desert often used to take a number of cockerels with them as protection against Basilisks. In Iceland a creature similar to the Basilisk is called a Skoffin.

Basilisk from a 13th century bestiary.

BEHEMOTH

Behemoth is a large and powerful monster described in The Book of Job in the Bible.

Behold now behemoth, which I made with thee; he ea-
teth grass as an ox.

Lo now, his strength is in his loins, and his force is in
the navel of his belly.

He moveth his tail like a cedar: the sinews of his stones
are wrapped together.

His bones are as strong as pieces of brass; his bones are
like bars of iron.

... Behold he drinketh up a river and hasteth not; he
trusteth that he can draw up Jordan into his mouth.

He taketh it with his eyes; his nose pierceth through
snares"

Its name is the plural of the Hebrew 'behemah' which means beast, the plural here is used in an augmentative sense. Pictorially he is represented as a creature similar to a water buffalo or a hippopotamus, a shape probably derived from the Egyptian hippopotamus goddess Taueret. This was the way that William Blake illustrated Behemoth in his drawings for the Book of Job. This monster is reputed to be seven miles long, who daily grazed upon a thousand miles of grass in Paradise. Behemoth symbolizes the power of the land as opposed to Leviathan, the power of the sea. Sometimes Behemoth contends with his deadliest enemy Leviathan and on the day of judgement these two are destined to slay each other.

Behemoth from a 12th century MS.

BONNACON

This Asian creature was also known as a Bonachus. Gaius Plinius Secundus (Pliny the Elder) in his book of natural history called it a Bonasus. He described it as bull-like but with the mane of a horse and horns that curved backwards and were so convoluted that they were no use in fighting. Other sources describe the Bonnacon as having a long hairy coat and green horns curled round like ammonites.

Although its horns were of no practical use, the Bonnacon was able to defend itself as, when it ran away from its enemies, the beast emitted a trail of dung behind it in such quantity that there was enough to cover a furlong of land. The excrement burnt up everything that it touched and charred to death any enemy that pursued the Bonnacon.

A Bonnacon.

BULL

See also Lamassu, Minotaur

The Bull is associated with the second sign of the zodiac, Taurus, and is an animal that symbolizes both sacrifice and victory; it also denotes the functions of fecundation and creation. These two aspects of the creature are clearly seen in Mithraic thought and ritual where, according to Cumont in 'Les Mysteres de Mithra' :-

> *"... out of his body grew all the plants and herbs that*
> *adorn the earth with verdure, and from his seed*
> *sprang all the animal species."*

Usually the Bull is regarded as a lunar symbol and the victory of the solar Lion over the Bull generally signifies the victory of day over night. But symbolically the Bull may also represent the spring equinox for, notably in Chaldean sculpture, two animals that can be found together, usually fighting, are the One Horned Bull – said to be the original unicorn – and a lion. As the lion is always the winner, it is thought that the bull represents the spring equinox which has to give way to the lion who is the symbol of the summer solstice. In some religions, a bull was sacrificed at new year marking the death of winter and the creative resurgence of spring.

Strictly speaking the Egyptian Apis Bull was not a mythological beast but an actual animal; it is the imagery surrounding the Apis that makes it fabulous. It was believed to have been conceived by a ray of moonlight falling upon a specially selected cow (a bull was considered to be related to the moon because of the crescent shape of its horns and because, in some primitive religions the moon is often male and its semen is the fecundating principle). The beast who was to become the Apis was recognized at birth by the markings on its body. It had to be black with a white triangle on its forehead and the shape of a crescent moon on its right flank.

Each individual Egyptian god was credited with powers that were unique to him and the High God Ptah needed a mediator to proclaim his heavenly will. The Sacred Bull was considered to be a messenger of the god Ptah and lived in the forecourt of his temple at Memphis. The priests of the temple noted the movements that the bull made during the course of the day and used them as a form of divination to interpret the wishes of their god. It remained in the temple precincts until it died of old age. The bull was then embalmed like a king and buried in a large tomb known as a Serapeum. A search was then conducted for his successor. In life, the Apis was worshipped as the reincarnation and servant of the artesian god Ptah and, after its death, was

A drawing of Taurus from 'Stars and Marvels of the East', a 12th century AD manuscript.

A 'Satirical Papyrus of the Egyptian Book of the Dead' shows a one-horned bull.

The Tarw Elgan from 'The Mabin of the Mabinogion'.

Winged bull from 'The Book of Kells'.

assimilated into the god Osiris.

Not everyone agreed that it died of old age. J. B. Frazer in his book "The Golden Bough" says that the bull was sacrificed by being drowned in a holy cistern when it reached the age of twenty five. The Apis was one of three sacred Egyptian Bulls, the others were called Mnevis or Merwer, and Buchis who lived in temples at Heliopolis and Hermon respectively. According to Morien O'Morgan, the Tarw Elgan, the White Sun Bull of the Druids, is contemporary with the Egyptian Apis Bull.

Some fabulous Bulls were tainted with evil and the Bull of Inde and Gudanna were both considered malevolent. The Bull of Inde was a cruel and evil Indian creature. It had yellow hair that grew in a tangled mass over an impenetrable hide, its horns were not fixed but moveable and it would commit suicide when captured.

When Gilgamesh, in Sumerian mythology, refused the love of the Goddess Ishtar, she persuaded Anu to create Gudanna, the Bull of Heaven, to destroy Gilgamesh's kingdom. The hero destroyed and dismembered the bull, helped by his wildman friend Enkidu but the Gods decreed that Enkidu should die for his part in the battle. These brutes differed in temperament from the Japanese Kurdan who had a man's head, horns along its back and three eyes on each of its flanks; it would never tell a lie.

The winged bull or calf is the Christian symbol of St. Luke where it represents the fixed element of earth and is linked with the imagery of the tetramorph. Giraldus Cambrensis wrote of the bull or calf of St. Luke in "Topographia Hiberniae" where he described a picture in a book that was probably *The Book of Kells* :-

> "Here the mystic symbols of the Evangelists, each with wings, now six, now four, now two, here the Eagle, there the Calf, here the Man and there the Lion, and other forms almost infinite."

BUNYIP

The Bunyip, known also as the Tunatabah and King Pratie, is a fabulous creature that has its home in Australia. It is dark-coloured and lives in deep pools or streams where it makes a sound like a loud booming roar. Anyone stupid enough to harm a young Bunyip lives to regret it for its mother immediately causes a great flood and anyone splashed by the floodwater changes into a black swan. In Tasmania, the Bunyip is a mythical giant snake – the Good Hoop or Universal Eye.

A Caladrius with its head turned away. A manuscript painting.

CALADRIUS

Many bestiaries describe the Caladrius as a white bird without even one speck of black upon it; it has a swan-like neck, a yellow beak and legs of the same colour. This bird is welcomed throughout Christendom and is found even in the halls of kings for it has remarkable powers of prognostication in disease. It will fly into the room of a sick person and, if it turns its head away and will not look at the patient, that person will die. If the illness is not mortal, the Caladrius will look at the invalid and take the sickness upon itself. It flies up towards the sun and vomits the infirmity into the air and the patient is thus cured. Rich living among the nobles of the middle ages resulted in attacks of jaundice and the Caladrius became associated with this disease.

Some bestiaries compare the Caladrius with Jesus Christ, for Christ will have no dealings with people who are mortally sick in spirit. The Roxburgh Bestiary, translated by T. H. White, states that Christ is likened to a Caladrius because Our Lord is entirely white having nothing black about him. He turns his face from the Jews because of their unbelief but bears the infirmities of believers upon himself and carries away their sins.

The Caladrius has been assumed to be many different kinds of bird, everything from a seagull to a white parrot. T. H. White was of the opinion that it was a white wagtail for wagtails are still regarded in Ireland with superstitious dread. However, the general consensus was that it was only a river bird.

In a "Bestiarie D'Amour" a lady who turned her head away from her suitor's attentions was reproached by him for acting like a Caladrius. She retorted that it was safer to do so as she did not wish to take the man's ills upon herself and exclaimed, "May the good God guard me from conceiving anything which would be dangerous to bring forth."

24

Previous page

**"The Caladrius foretells
that the king will live."
From a medieval
manuscript painting.**

**Kwakiutl Cannibal bird
mask of The Crooked Beak
of Heaven.**

CANNIBAL BIRDS

The Cannibal Birds are to be found in the mythology of
the North American Indian tribes. These birds figure in the
ceremonial dances of the Indians of the Canadian Northwest where incidents from hereditary family myths are
portrayed. The Hamatsa, roughly translated as 'cannibal', is
the dance drama that features Bakhbakwalanooksiway – the
Cannibal at the North End of the World – and his fabulous
bird monster metamorphoses into forms of the Raven and
the Hokhiku. Hokhoku has a long thin beak with which he
crushes men's skulls in order to eat their brains and the
Raven, known as Gwagwakhwalanooksiwey eats men's
eyeballs. His wife, Galokwudzuwis, can also change her
form and becomes The Crooked Beak of Heaven, identified
by the crooked appendage on her upper beak. The forms of
Raven and Hokhoku are worn by the Cannibal at the North
End of the World when he hunts to obtain food and his wife
transforms herself into The Crooked Beak of Heaven in
order to accompany him. In the dark stormy days of autumn
Bakhbakwalanooksiway travels south to hunt and appears
before his terrified victims emitting his ominous cry of
"Hap! Hap!" (Eat! Eat!)

In the Hamatsa, a novice from a local village is kidnapped
by the Cannibal and taken to his great house, in the mountains, at the North End of the World where red smoke can
be seen issuing from the roof. Here Bakhbakwalanooksiway
transforms the boy into his own spirit in the form of a wild
man-eater. The novice is then returned to his village where

he has to be captured and tamed by means of song and dance. In the dance drama, monster bird masks with great snapping jaws representing the Cannibal birds are worn by dancers during part of the ritual.

CAPRICORNUS

Capricorn is the tenth sign of the traditional zodiac and its symbol is Capricornus, the Goat-fish, the sign of the winter solstice, the Janua Coeli or the ascending power of the sun.

The Goat-fish has straight or curved horns on a goat's head, the front half of a goat and the rear body of a fish with a tail fin. The symbol of Capricorn is a simplified drawing of the body; the curling flourish at the end being its fish tail. This combination of goat and fish represents the dual nature of land and sea and, as it unites a mountain goat with a deep sea fish, it also shows the duality of height and depth. In Hindu doctrine, the duality of this sign signifies the involutive and the evolutive possibilities; the return to or departure from the zodiacal wheel of rebirth.

The Goat-fish is a creature of early Mesopotamian origin. It was one of the attributes of the God Ea, Lord of the Abyss, who ruled 'the waters under the earth'. The Babylonians called this amphibian sea god Oannes. He was said to have been born out of a great egg, a common theme in creation myths. In a surviving fragment of the 'Babylonian History', written by a priest called Berossus, Oannes was described as having the head and body of a fish; under the head of the fish he had a human head and feet similar to those of a man were subjoined to the fish's tail. He was reputed to have taught the Sumerians the arts of mathematics, astronomy and agriculture.

One of the fixed star constellations in the path of the sun is that of Capricorn and one story tells that Zeus changed the Goat God Pan into the constellation of Capricorn when he leapt into the Nile while endeavouring to escape from the monster Typhon. Pan was trying to change completely into a goat when he leapt into the water but was given a fish tail in order to survive. Capricornus is also known as a Ram-fish and its Sumerian name was 'Suhur-mas' meaning carp-goat.

CATOBLEPAS

Pliny the Elder was the first person to mention the Catoblepas and described it as a sluggish creature of moderate size that lived to the south of Egypt on the borders of

The popular North American Indian Raven.

Capricornus from an ancient MS.

The solitary Catoblepas.

Ethiopia. Its head was so remarkably heavy that the beast had to carry it low to the ground which was fortunate for the human race for, should a man look into the eyes of a Catoblepas, he instantly fell down dead. The word 'catoblepas' in Greek means 'that which looks downwards'. It is thought that the Gnu may have been the animal that originally inspired the descriptions of this fabulous beast.

Edward Topsell, in the 17th century, described it as a beast set all over with scales like a dragon, with no hair on its body only on its head, great teeth like a swine, having wings but no will to fly, hands on the end of its legs, and was in stature between a bull and a calf. He called it a Gorgon.

Flaubert included the Catoblepas among the many strange animals that beset St. Anthony in his drama "The Temptation of St. Anthony":-

"Obese, downhearted, wary, I do nothing but feel under my belly the warm mud. My head is so heavy that I cannot bear its weight. I wind it slowly round my body; with half open jaws, I pull up with my tongue poisonous plants dampened by my breath. Once I ate my forelegs unawares. No one, Anthony, has ever seen my eyes; or else, those who have seen them have died. If I were to lift my eyelids – my pink and swollen eyelids – you would die on the spot."

CECROPS

Cecrops was the son of Mother Earth and Erechtheus, King of Attica and, like his father, was half man and half serpent. He had the body of a serpent from the waist downwards. Here the serpentine body does not signify an aspect of evil, like the monster Echidne, but represents fecundity, wisdom and guardianship of the springs of life. Cecrops ruled in Attica after his father's death and was reputed to be the first king to recognise paternity. He also banned the use of animal sacrifices and offered only barley cakes to the Gods.

CENTAUR

The Centaur is one of the most ancient of the Fabulous Beasts. Early illustrations of it have been found in Assyria dating from the 2nd millennium BC and in India from the 3rd Millennium BC. It is said that Centaurs are derived from the Gandharvas who, in Vedic mythology, drove the horses of the sun.

Cecrops, King of Attica.

Centaurs are portrayed with the head and body from the navel upwards of a man set upon the body and legs of a horse. However there are a number of different types of Centaur. 'The Physiologus', the nickname of an anonymous author who wrote a book which was the ancestor of medieval bestiaries, described Onocentaurs as having a human head, arms and torso, and the lower parts of an ass. Ichthyocentaurs are water beasts with the tail of a dolphin and the forelegs of a horse or lion. The Apotharni were a tribe of half horse half human creatures whose females were bald and bearded and the Scythian Ipopodes were human apart from their legs and feet which were equine. Occasionally the Centaur's lower body is that of a lion or some other wild beast.

The most well known Centaurs are those found in Greek Mythology; their birth was magical. Ixion, son of the Lapith King, planned to seduce the Goddess Hera but was forestalled by her husband Zeus who transformed a cloud into the shape of the Goddess. Ixion was deceived and made love to the cloud woman who was afterwards called Nephele. She bore Ixion a child – Centaurus – who is said to have sired Horse-centaurs on Magnesian mares.

The king of the Centaurs was the immortal Cheiron who was described as the most just of beings. He was renowned for his wisdom and his skill in the arts of medicine, music and archery and taught these skills to the hero Achilles. Unfortunately, Heracles accidentally wounded Cheiron in

12th century image of Sagittarius. From the monastery of Sacra di San Michele, Italy.

A lion-bodied Centaur. From a roof boss in Westminster Abbey, England.

Centaur and dragon in Adel Parish Church, England.

the foot with one of his poisoned arrows and, in great pain, Cheiron surrendered his immortality to Prometheus in order to escape from everlasting agony. Zeus fixed his image in the sky as the constellation Sagittarius and the symbol of the ninth sign of the traditional zodiac (Sagittarius) is a centaur holding a bow and arrow.

A member of the Centaur family that was akin to Cheiron was the Sumerian Bucentaur Hea Bani. He had the head, body and arms of a man and the rest of his body and legs were those of a bull. Like Cheiron he was celebrated for his wisdom.

Centaurs were famous for their lustfulness. For example, the Centaur Nessus was killed by Heracles when he attempted to abscond with the hero's wife Deianeira, and when the Centaurs were invited to the wedding of Peirithous the Lapith, and Hippodameia, they became intoxicated and lecherously attacked the women present. In the ensuing fight the Centaurs were defeated.

In Christian symbolism the centaur is a sign of sensuality, passion and adultery and the man/horse can often be seen carved into church decorations where it is the symbol of man's higher instincts being destroyed by his animal appetites.

CERBERUS
See also Dog

Cerberus, the multi-headed watchdog of the Underworld
– the guardian of dead souls who prevents their return into
the world above – was the offspring of the storm God
Typhon and the serpent Goddess Echidne. Hesiod, in his
'Theogony', wrote that Cerberus had fifty heads; Pindar and
Horace said that she had a hundred but she is usually
illustrated with three heads, a dragon's neck and a back and
tail bristling with serpents heads. The three heads relate to
the threefold symbols of the baser forces of life; they are the
infernal replica of the divine triunity.

Like the serpent/dragons associated with the oracles,
Cerberus would be offered honey cakes, 'a sop to Cerberus',
by the souls of the dead in the Underworld to ensure their
safe passage. One of the Labours of Heracles was his 'Har-
rowing of Hell'. He had to capture Cerberus in the House of
Hades on the banks of the Stygian lake and drag her into the
light of the land of the living. As he hauled Cerberus, bound
with adamantine chains, up from the Underworld, barking
furiously, wherever her slaver dripped from her jaws upon
the ground, there grew the poisonous plant Aconite. Dante
described Cerberus as "Il gran vermo inferno" thus linking
her with the legendary worms and orms. In Norse mythology the dog Garm or Garmr guards the House of the Dead.

Many-headed Cerberus,
from a Greek hydria.

CH'I-LIN

The Ch'i-lin or Ki-lin, also known in Japan as the Kirin, is
one of the four spiritually endowed Chinese creatures. The
others are the Tortoise, the Dragon and the Fêng Hwang.
The Ch'i-lin is reputed to be the leader of all the creatures
that live on the land and is the incarnate essence of the five
elements: fire, water, metal, wood and earth.

The Ch'i or Ki is the male and Lin is the female animal. It
is shaped like a large deer with the tail of an ox, the hooves
of a horse and a single horn on its head. Because of this
horn and the pure nature of the beast, the Ch'i-lin is considered to be the oriental equivalent of the Unicorn. It has a
multi-coloured coat, its back is coloured red, yellow, blue,
white and black while its stomach is brown or yellow. The
cry of the Ch'i-lin sounds like a peal of bells and, as it can
hardly ever be captured or slain, it is reputed to live for 1000
years. It will never eat anything living and will not even put
its hooves on growing grass. According to the 'Bamboo

A metal sculpture of a
Ch'i-lin.

Chronicle' the Ch'i-lin is considered to be the noblest of all the creatures of the animal kingdom.

This glorious creature represents peace, prosperity and good fortune, and is the emblem of the upright Judge or Emperor symbolizing a just ruler who spares the innocent but punishes the guilty; its horn is said to be the weapon of punishment. The Chi'-lin is an attribute of high ranking officials and used to be depicted on their caps as a symbol of justice. When the Ch'i-lin is seen abroad in the land, it is a sign of the virtue of the reigning monarch and shows that his judgement has achieved an ideal balance in support of cosmic order. It is claimed that the Ch'i-lin first appeared during the reign of the Emperor Huang-ti (2697-2597 BC) and also foretold the birth of Confucius by appearing and spitting out a piece of jade which bore the words.

*"Son of mountain crystal, when the dynasty crumbles
thou shalt rule as a throneless king."*

CHIMERA

See also Pegasus

The Chimera, like Cerberus, was the offspring of Echidne, the serpent woman, and Typhon – one of the largest monsters ever born. She was the mother of the Nemean Lion and the Sphinx; Orthrus, the Dog Star, was said to be their father.

Homer described her as having a lion's foreparts, a goat in the middle and a serpent's hindparts. She is sometimes depicted with three heads. A famous Etruscan bronze of the fifth century BC shows the head of a lion on a body that has

The Etruscan bronze of the Chimera showing the lion, goat and serpent.

a goat's head sprouting from its back and a tail with a serpent's head on the end. In the late middle ages she was sometimes illustrated with the face of a beautiful young maiden. The Chimera is a symbol of complex evil.

This savage creature was the household pet of the King of Caria and caused havoc in Lydia by killing everyone who came in range of its fiery breath. She was eventually slain by Bellerophon, mounted on his winged horse Pegasus, who managed to insert a lump of lead into her jaws where her fiery breath melted the metal and allowed it to trickle down her throat.

It has been said that the Chimera was a figurative description of a mountain in Lycia, a volcanic but fertile place. Its summit was the lair of lions, the middle was a pasture for goats and its foothills were infested by serpents.

Robert Graves in 'The Greek Myths' is of the opinion that this creature is a Carian Calendar Beast; the lion represents spring, the goat is summer and the serpent is winter. In recent times the Chimera is regarded as the embodiment of extravagant fantasy. Nowadays the phrase 'to chase a Chimera' is used when anyone wishes to indulge in useless flights of fancy.

Cockatrice eggs.

COCKATRICE

See also Amphisbaena, Basilisk, Wyvern

The Cockatrice is closely linked to the Basilisk. The travellers in North Africa, who took a cock with them as protection against Basilisks, began describing a new and different type of Basilisk which had the head of a cock. This creature was at first called a Basilcock and later a Cockatrice.

A very curious history was attributed to the Cockatrice. It had to be born from a toughened, shell-less egg laid by a seven year old cock bird during the days of Sirius the dog star. The egg was spherical, not ovoid, and had to be hatched out by a toad or a snake on a dung heap. The Cockatrice that sprang forth from this egg was winged with the body of a cock or wyvern but always with a wyvern's tail. Both body and tail were yellow and sometimes the tail had an extra head at its tip which was just as poisonous as the main head. The eyes, that still retained their murderous Basilisk stare, resembled those of a toad. To the medieval Christians, the cockatrice represented sin and sudden death, and was one of the four aspects of the devil.

A Cockatrice based on an illustration from Johann Stabius' "De Labyrintho".

CROCOTTA
See also Leucrota

This derivation of the hyaena species was recorded in Ctesias' compilation of a history of India made in the 4th century BC. In this book he wrote an account of the Cynolycus which he likened to a wolf-dog. Pliny took this description and gave it the name Crocotta adding that this mating of a wolf with a dog had produced a creature that could break anything with its teeth. The Corocotta, Crocotte, or Crocuta is a similar creature but is described as a cross between a hyena and a lioness.

CYNOCEPHALIC

There are two types of Cynocephalic, only one of which is fabulous. In the Egyptian 'Book of the Dead', or to give it its more accurate title the 'Book of Going Forth by Day', one type is an actual monkey which is the symbol of dawn. It has probably become associated with this symbol because the cynocephalic monkey wakes anyone within its vicinity with its strident call before dawn.

The other type, the fabulous Cynocephalics (which in Greek means 'dogheads') were called by this name because their heads were actually those of dogs. Ctesias gave a description of them as human bodied with horse's necks and dog heads. Herodotus said that they lived in Ethiopia. They could spit out fire from their mouths and did not talk, but barked their communications.

Marco Polo, the Italian explorer, wrote that they inhabited the Andaman Islands in the Andaman Sea, off the coast of Burma. They engaged in peaceful trade with India and, although they sometimes devoured human flesh, their diet was rice, apples, nuts and milk. In the book of his travels Sir John Mandeville described them as living on the Isle of Macumeran, a location no longer known. Their king was identified by a huge ruby pendant around his neck and his subjects worshipped an ox and wore its image on their turbans.

The dog-headed Cynocephalic.

The Black Dog also known as the Padfoot, Barguest or Shrike.

DOG

See also Cerberus

Dogs are the emblems of faithfulness and are considered to be the guardians and shepherds of flocks, but in mythology there is a darker side to their symbolism for they are also the guardians of the spirits of the dead when they make their 'Night Sea Crossing'. The pack of hounds that accompany the shadowy Gwyn ap Nudd, Celtic warder of the Underworld, on his wild hunt are known by many names including the Gabriel Hounds, the Hounds of Hell, Gabriel Ratchet Hounds, the Seven Whistlers and the Irish Hounds. It is said that the hounds chase the souls of the damned across the stormy sky at night and that to hear even the sound of the hunt means death. These Hounds of Hell with terrifying fiery eyes and a savage howl would drag sinners down into the underworld. However, it was more fortunate to encounter the Hounds of Heaven for their bell-like cry informed their victim that he would only be dragged back to repentance. In Norse mythology, the God Odin chased his prey across the sky followed by his pack of baying hounds. One story about the hounds and their huntsman tells that a mortal is instantly transported to another place if he is caught by the hunt, but has to remain silent about the huntsman or face death.

In the British Isles there are many legends about Black Dogs; these include the Barguest, Padfoot or Shrike. The shaggy coated beasts, with fiery eyes the size of saucers, are goblin dogs and their ghostly noctambulations across the moors are accompanied by wailing voices and the clanking of chains. It is the advance warning of death to hear the padding of the Black Dog's feet drawing

34

nearer for, if one of these dogs approaches a mortal, that person instantly becomes dumb and dies.

The Cir Sith is the hound who guards fairy knowes in the Scottish Isles. It is coloured green, and has a long tail coiled up on its back. It chases travellers, making a noise like that of a galloping horse, and kills them mercilessly. The Ce Sith is a similar dog found in the Scottish Highlands. The T'ien Kou is even more terrifying. There is only one T'ien Kou – the Chinese Celestial Dog – alive at any one time. This is just as well for the huge creature, with an appetite for children and human liver, is an omen of destruction and catastrophe. When it descends from its home in the night sky to the earth, it resembles a comet with a tail of fire. It is the demon of meteors and eclipses.

In comparison, the other types of monstrous dog seem mild. A large Chilean dog called a Calchona is white and woolly with a long beard. It seeks out travellers at night, snatches their lunch boxes and retreats with the food muttering frightening curses. The Qiqion, an inhabitant of North America, will cause an Eskimo that catches a glimpse of it to fall into a fit. This dog has hair only on its mouth, ears, feet and the tip of its tail.

Two much more attractive little dogs are the Dogs of Fo and the Mimicke Dog. The Chinese Lion Dogs also known as The Dogs of Fo are portrayed in paintings and sculptures with lion's bodies and bushy tails. They occasionally have wings and sometimes a single horn. They are seen as guardian figures and are generally depicted in pairs. The female has a puppy under her paw and the male rests one of his front legs on a ball; some dogs have both these embellishments. Guardian figures, like these, are found facing each other in pairs because the reassurance of symmetry is a strong ingredient of protective magic.

The friendly and attractive little Mimicke Dog can imitate anything. It has a hairy coat and a pointed little snout. It was believed to be common in Egypt in Ptolemy's time where it was trained by apes to take the place of servants in the homes of poor people.

DRACONIOPIDES

See also Serpent

Lilith appears, in Hebrew legend, as a night phantom and the enemy of newly born babies. She is the sign of the fearsome aspects of the Terrible Mother who represents not only death but indifference towards human suffering. An

Mimicke Dog based on the drawing in Edward Topsell's 'Historie of Foure-footed Beasts'.

A Sea Dog.

Opposite

Dog of Fo and puppy. A ceramic sculpture.

old Hebrew text states "For before Eve was Lilith" and in some Hebrew literature she was described as the first wife of Adam who refused to lie beneath him and obey his commands. When Adam spurned Lilith and married Eve in the Garden of Eden, she revenged herself on Adam's wife by persuading her to eat the forbidden fruit.

It is likely that Lilith represented the female deity that was worshipped before the male-orientated religion of Judaism took its place. One of the best known symbols of the Goddess was a serpent and in Rome the Goddess Isis was depicted as a human-headed snake. This tradition was continued in medieval times when Lilith was shown coiled about the Tree of Knowledge, with the head of a beautiful woman and the body of a serpent, tempting Eve with the apple. This composite creature is known as a Draconiopides.

According to the Zohar, the leading book of Jewish Kabbalism, the serpent in the Garden of Eden was a kind of flying camel, a creature which was traditionally considered to be related to flying dragons.

DRAGON

See also Amphisbaena, Hydra, Wyvern, Tiāmat

The Dragon is the most famous and possibly the oldest of all the Fabulous Beasts and this universal and symbolic figure is found in the majority of cultures throughout the world, primitive, classical, medieval and oriental. The names 'Drakon' and 'Draco' were used throughout the Greek and Roman Empires to describe a large snake and the word Dragon is derived from both of these names. In ancient times dragon and serpent mythology were closely interwoven and it was only much later in history that the dragon and the snake separated. To read the early history of the Western Dragon, turn to the sections on the Serpent and the Worm. Information about the Eastern Dragon can be found under the heading Oriental Dragon.

The Western Dragon has been described as the most venerable symbol employed in ornamental art. Pictures of this awe- inspiring beast, twisting its body in graceful and intricate coils, make very decorative works of art. This can be seen in the worldwide distribution of paintings, drawings and sculptures of the creature, which gives a comprehensive representation of all the stages of a Dragon's career from its birth out of an egg lying at the bottom of the sea to its death often at the hands of a hero. Therefore, it is not easy

Opposite
Draconopides. From Ulm Cathedral, Germany. 1420.

Lilith. Part of a woodcut. Augsberg 1470

An Aspis from a medieval bestiary.

A Fertility Dragon with a vine growing from its mouth.

A maiden changing into a Dragon.

to describe the appearance of a Dragon for nearly every artist illustrates him in a different way. One is shown with a red scaly armour-plated body and fiery breath while another is described as black with its body all puffed up with poison and trailing a snail-like, slimy secretion. Puk, a German household Dragon, was a small quadruped and the Safat was a winged creature with a fierce dragon's head. The Aspis was a small, two-legged dragon that was so venomous that a bite or even a touch ensured certain death; only music had the power to charm it. The Aspis was so sensitive to music that, in order to avoid being overcome, it stopped up one ear with the tip of its tail and pressed the other ear to the ground. In Western cultures, however, a general description of a dragon would be that it had four legs, a long serpentine body with a barbed tail, a fierce wyvern's head, ribbed wings and sharp claws and teeth.

The Greek word 'Drakon' comes from a verb meaning 'to see' or 'to watch' and Dragons have great reputations as guardians of wisdom, treasure and the virtue of maidens entrusted to their care. From Aelian's "De Natura Animalium" comes the story of the guardian Dragons who lived in a sacred grove in Lavinium. Sacred virgins had to present barley cakes to one of the resident Dragons. This was a test of the girl's virtue for, if the girl was impure, the Dragon would refuse to eat the cake. Today a conscientious duenna may be described as a Dragon, an unconscious tribute to her vigilance.

In Greek Mythology the Dragon Ladon guarded the apples on the Tree of the Hesperides for the Goddess Hera. Ladon, who was said to be the parthenogenous son of Mother Earth, was multiple-headed like the Persian Dragon Thu'bān. He had a hundred heads and, with two hundred keen-sighted eyes, he was the obvious choice for a guardian. However, even with these advantages, he was no match for the hero Heracles who shot the Dragon with an arrow and stole the apples. To commemorate this feat, Heracles bore the likeness of a Dragon on his shield which was described by Homer as:-

"A scaly horror of a Dragon, coiled full in the central
    field, unspeakable, with eyes oblique, retorted, that
    askant shot gleaming fire."

The Goddess Hera wept bitterly at the death of Ladon and set his image among the stars as the constellation of the serpent Draco. Draco, also known as the Red Dragon, is a circumpolar constellation of stars which can be seen in the northern sky. In the Chaldean configuration Draco was a much longer and more serpentine beast than it is today.

Nowadays in Astronomical charts, his tail coils round the two bears and his head lies under the foot of Heracles.

There are also guardian Dragons in Norse mythology. Fafnir was a Dragon who guarded a pile of gold and Hordeshyrde was the warden of a great treasure until he fought and was slain by Beowulf, King of the Geats.

The original Dragon was mainly a beneficient creature who never forgot its beginnings by always displaying a strong affinity for water, the lifeblood of the land. It was universally associated with the regenerative powers of water that rise from the depths of the earth to give fertility to the soil. It is, therefore, not surprising that Dragons are intimately connected with earth goddesses in particular and women in general. In early Mediterranean art, the Great Goddess is often shown in the company of a dragon. There is a cylinder seal in existence from the Tigris Euphrates valley, inhabited as early as 4,000 BC by the Sumerians, which shows the Great Goddess Bau on the left of the tree of life. Behind her rears a great serpent dragon representing her lifegiving powers. Ceres, the earth goddess, had a chariot drawn by two dragons which she lent to Triptolemus giving him a bag of seed with which to teach agriculture to the world.

Stonecarving of St. Margaret bursting the Dragon.

In 'The Travels of Sir John Mandeville' the story is related of a lady who was changed from a fair maiden into a great dragon. She was fated to remain in this monstrous form until a knight arrived who was brave enough to kiss her on the mouth. Two knights who saw her awful appearance fled away in fear and another, who knew that she would not harm him, still could not bring himself to touch her face. She still remains in the shape of a dragon waiting for a knight bold enough to approach her.

In Christian countries the Dragon has been regarded as the apotheosis of evil. Depictions show an amalgam of elements taken from various dangerous and aggressive animals thus making it a symbol of 'things animal' par excellence and a creature that was considered to be the supreme adversary with whom combat was the greatest test. The Dragon was the evil that Saints had to conquer; in many churches there are masterpieces of hagiography, depictions of St. Michael and St. George slaying the monster in combat, St. Margaret bursting it asunder with her crucifix and St. Martha defeating the dragon Tarasque by sprinkling it with holy water. Medieval artists drew the Gates of Hell as a Dragon's mouth open to receive the damned and in the Apocalypse it is described as *"that old serpent, which is the Devil and Satan"* whose tail *"drew the third part of the stars of*

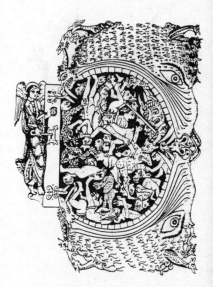

A Dragon as 'The Gate of Hell'. From 'The Winchester Psalter.'

A windsock Dragon.
Historisches Archiv, Codex
W. Cologne, Germany.
15th century.

The Welsh Dragon.

Opposite

Merlin and King Arthur's
Dragon.

Heaven and did cast them to the earth". Teillard said that present day psychology defines the dragon symbol as "something terrible to overcome" for only he who conquers a dragon becomes a hero.

The heraldic Dragon, unlike its medieval counterpart, does not symbolize evil. When it is seen on banners, standards and shields, it is a sign of valour and represents the power of a ruler. The dragon windsock banner was a familiar sight in the time of the Roman Empire. The Persians and the Scythians bore dragons on their standards and it is possible that the Romans copied the design of these banners. These windsock standards were among the chief insignia of the Roman armies. A windsock consisted of a pole, held by a soldier called a Dragonarius, which had a carved wooden Dragon's head mounted on top of it. A tube of cloth was attached to the head and, when the banner was held aloft, it filled with wind, writhing and billowing like a living creature. The fierce appearance of these banners – some windsocks appeared very realistic – had the effect of terrifying the enemy as well as assisting the archers by showing them the strength and direction of the wind.

The legend of the creation of the Welsh flag tells how King Vortigern was unable to build a fortress at Dinas Emrys because the stonework of its foundations kept collapsing. Merlin explained to the King that the reason that the building kept falling was because two dragons were fighting in a lake underneath the fortress and shaking its walls. Excavations were carried out and the truth of Merlin's prophesy was shown by the discovery of a red Dragon, representing the Britons, and a white Dragon, symbol of the Saxons, fighting in a subterranean lake beneath the castle. The red Dragon won and became the emblem of Wales. Y ddraig goch ddyry cychwyn (The Red Dragon gives impetus) is the badge of Wales. In later years Merlin became the chief adviser and magician to King Arthur, son of Uther Pendragon. Uther had a vision of a flaming Dragon which was interpreted by his sorcerers as a sign that he would become king. He took the name of Pendragon which means "head Dragon" and this became the title of an overlord while Dragon became the title of a chief. Arthur also participated in this symbolism and is often depicted wearing a Dragon on his helm to indicate his rank.

In alchemy, a number of Dragons fighting each other illustrates psychic disintegration or the separating out of the elements. Winged Dragons stand for the volatile elements and wingless represent the fixed.

42

A Double-headed Eagle which was the emblem of Imperial Germany, Russia and Austria.

EAGLE

The Eagle is the most famous symbol of all aerial creatures and is credited with the power to be able to look at the sun without scorching its eyes. Like the sun, it represents fire and light.

The double-headed Eagle has the same symbolism as the two-headed Janus figure, the co-joining of the spiritual and the temporal, the knowledge of both the past and the future, and the duplication of power. It was once thought that the emblem of the two-headed Eagle originated in heraldry; in the dimidiation (dimidiation was effected by the division of a shield down the middle) upon one shield of two separate coats of arms. In A. C. Fox Davies 'Complete Guide to Heraldry', he states that Nisbet concluded that the Imperial Double-Headed Eagle of Germany was not one creature with two heads but two birds facing opposite ways, each representing one part of the Empire when it was divided into east and west. However, the two-headed eagle was known long before heraldry came into existence, for the Hittites used this symbol as their national badge and in Sumero-Semitic mythology the Double-headed Eagle is the symbol of Nergal, the scorching heat of the noonday summer sun, and is also an attribute of twin gods.

In alchemy the double-headed Eagle is usually depicted in two colours of great mystical significance, red and white; the Eagle devouring a lion represents the volatilization of the fixed.

ECHIDNE

See also Melusine, Vouivre

Chrysaor, the daughter of Medusa, gave birth to Echidne, the snake maiden, within a deep, hollowed-out cave. Echidne was a monster with the upper half of a fair-faced nymph of seductive and alluring manner. Unfortunately, her lower half was that of a serpent; terrible, great, spotted and ravenous. She grew up in her cave and used her beautiful head and torso to lure men to her but, when they were trapped, her serpent nature took over and she ate them raw. Echidne mated with the storm god Typhon and her offspring included Cerberus, the guardian of the Underworld, the Chimera and the many-headed Hydra. She was killed, while she slept, by the hundred-eyed Argus Panoptes. Echidne's role is that of the monstrous mother image, devouring and incestuous. In Christian symbolism, she is the notorious prostitute whose visible attractions do not conceal her shameful lower nature.

Echidna, magnetic but deadly, half serpent and half maiden.

EEL

See also Midgard's Worm, Worm

The Eel partially shares the symbolism of the Serpent and, in some cases the Worm. The Jinshin Uwo, like Midgard's Worm, supports the weight of the earth but, in this case, Japan is the only country that it bears upon its back. It is seven hundred miles long with its head resting beneath Kyoto and its tail below Awomori. When it lashes its tail, it causes earthquake tremors throughout the country.

The Abaia, a great eel of Melanesian mythology, loved the fish who shared his lake so much that he caused a deluge if any of them were caught.

The Burach Bhadi, also known as the Wizard's Shackle, lives in the Western Isles of Scotland. It is an eel or leech with nine squinting eyes and a horrible habit of entwining itself around a horse's legs, pulling the animal down to die in the waters of the ford where it lives.

ERINNYES

The Erinnyes, the Furies, were the daughters of Uranus and the Mother Goddess of the Earth. The Goddess persuaded her son Cronus to castrate his father Uranus but some spots of blood dropped from the wounded God and fell upon Mother Earth who thereupon conceived the three Erinnyes. The Erinnyes, the Angry Ones, were described in Greek Mythology as the three crones Tisiphone, Alecto and Megaera who had snakes for hair, dog's heads, dark bodies, bats' wings, and bloodshot eyes. They carried brass-studded scourges to beat their victims. They personified remorse in the sense that they symbolize guilt which is turned to destructive tendencies towards the guilty party; they represented the pangs of conscience and punished

An oriental jade carving of an eel-like creature.

The savage and pitiless
Erinnyes.

crimes of parricide and perjury. A man who breaks their
taboos will die either by committing suicide in a fit of
madness or he will refuse food and drink until he starves to
death. The snaky hair and dog's head show that these ap-
paritions were of an infernal nature and should be regarded
as chthonic demons.

In mythology, they attacked Orestes after he had slain his
mother and her lover Aegisthus, in revenge for their murder
of his father Agamemnon. As punishment for his crime,
Orestes was sentenced to roam far away from home for a
year pursued and harried by the tireless Erinnyes. It was not
long before they caused the young man to lose his wits and,
although he did not die, he bit off his finger in an effort to
placate the vengeful beings. When the year was over, the
Gods acquitted Orestes. The fury of the Erinnyes at being
balked of their prey was appeased by being given hearth
altars and worship proper to Underworld deities. From that
time onwards they were known as the Solemn Ones, although some deny that the august matrons – worshipped
by that name – were ever these mad Goddesses.

A Falcon Fish with the pointed ears of a hound.

FALCON FISH

See also Merman, Capricornus

There was once a common belief that everything on earth was duplicated in the sea; the Hippocamp, the Mermaid and Capricornus (the goat-fish) are the clearest examples of this. Sylvester's translation of a poem written by Du Bartas (1578) reads :-

"Seas have...
Also Rams. Calfs, Horses, Hares and Hogs,
Wolves, Lions, Urchins, Elephants and Dogs,
Ye Men and Mayds: and (which I more admire)
The Mytred Bishop, and the Cowled Fryer."

Examples of these aquatic creatures can be seen in a number of church decorations like the ceiling painting of the Church of Zillis where such amphibians as the Fox-fish, fish-geese and the Unicorn-fish can be seen. The Falcon-fish should be included in this list. It has the foreparts of a bird with Griffon-like ears and the tail of a fish, and is also to be found in heraldry. Symbolically it can be seen as paralleling Capricornus, linking a solar bird of the heights (instead of a mountain climbing goat) with a piscine being of the depths.

FEATHERED SERPENT

Quetzalcoatl, the shining Lord of the Morning Star, was one of the most important figures in the religion of pre-Columbian Mexico. He was the

Mexican sculpture of
Quetzalcoatl rising out of
the serpent's jaws.

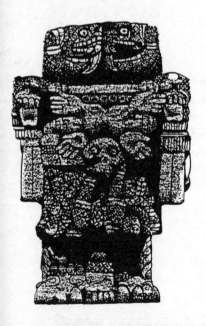

A sculpture of Coatlicue,
excavated from beneath the
cathedral square in Mexico
City in 1824.

astrological deity of the Morning Star who lifted up the Sun in the morning and controlled the winds, springtime and the rising growth of all plants succoured by the beneficial sunlight.

Some legends state that he was the son of the Earth Monster, a gigantic alligator-like reptile, who resided in the depths of the Great Waters. The Earth Monster was lured to the surface of the waters by the god Tezcatlipoca who used his own foot as bait. Tezcatlipoca lost his foot in the titanic battle that ensued, but he managed to tear off the monster's lower jaw preventing her from sinking back into the sea. Her great back became the earth – the birthplace of all mankind. The legend of Tezcatlipoca and the Earth Monster parallels that of the Babylonian dragoness Ti 50⁻amat and her conqueror Marduk.

Coatlicue, the Earth Mother, portrays another aspect of the Earth Monster; she was depicted with a head composed of rattlesnakes which were also on her garments. Rattlesnakes were the symbols of poverty for, as the world was made from the Earth Mother's body, she owned nothing.

The story of Quetzalcoatl, Lord of healing, relates how he came to earth and founded an empire among the people of Mexico becoming both their king and a celibate priest. He lived a holy and chaste life until he was tempted by the Goddess Tlazoteotl who offered him some magic mushrooms. Under their hallucinatory influence, he copulated with the Goddess. In despair, knowing that he had defiled and condemned himself, Quetzalcoatl left his palaces and travelled to the shores of the Caribbean Sea where he embarked, naked, on a raft of serpent skins and sailed towards the sunrise. The Sun's heat ignited the boat and Quetzalcoatl's incandescent heart flew up to join with the Sun.

As Quetzalcoatl is described as a sexually potent, i.e. fertile being, whose energies were not released until he was tempted by Tlazoteotl, he can be seen as a springtime and vegetation God akin to the other vegetation Gods who suffered death in order to promote the fertility of the land.

The Aztec feathered or plumed serpent is the major symbol of the God Quetzalcoatl and represents conscious thought and intelligence. It is a combination of the Quetzal bird and serpent, with the head and body of a serpent covered in Quetzal feathers. It is primarily a symbol of air. When the Lord of the Morning Star emerges in the morning, he comes forth out of the serpent that wears the feathers of the Quetzal bird.

The green feathered Quetzal, a native of Guatemala, is regarded as the most beautiful of all birds. Its name Quetzaltotolin means the most precious bird and Quetzalcoatl means the most precious serpent, but the word 'coatl' also means 'a twin' and here refers to a pair of stars, the Morning Star Quetzalcoatl and the Evening Star Xolotl; the name Quetzalcoatl can also mean 'precious twin'.

However, the God Quetzalcoatl is not the feathered serpent itself but the one who emerges from between its jaws just as the Morning Star appears over the horizon. There are a number of beautiful sculptures of Quetzalcoatl showing the face of the God in the serpent's jaws as he arises in the morning. Kukulcan is the Mayan equivalent of Quetzalcoatl.

FÊNG HWANG

See also Phoenix

The Fêng Hwang, the vermilion bird, is the Chinese form of the Phoenix. It is known in Japan as the Ho-o. The Fêng Hwang is the chief of all birds and is one of the four

Part of a K'o-ssu (a woven silk tapestry) showing a Fêng Hwang.

spiritually endowed Chinese creatures; the others are the Tortoise, the Ch'i-lin and the Dragon. There are both male and female birds, Yin and Yang. The female bird Hwang is Yin, lunar, representing beauty, delicacy of feeling and peace, for the Fêng Hwang is never seen in times of war. Fêng (the masculine bird is Yang) is solar and the bird of fire. It should be noted that when the Fêng Hwang is portrayed with the Dragon – the symbol of the Emperor – it is entirely feminine and the symbol of the Empress.

When the Fêng Hwang appears, it is a very auspicious sign and signifies peace, the coming of a great Sage, or it marks the humanitarian rule of an Emperor. Before the Yellow Emperor died, the Fêng Hwang and the Ch'i-lin showed themselves to mankind as evidence of the benevolence of the Emperor's rule.

The traditional description of this exalted bird gives it the head of a cock, the back of a swallow, its wings are the wind, its tail is formed of trees and flowers and its feet are the earth. It bears on its body the characters for virtue, righteousness, humanity, sincerity and integrity. Other sources describe it as having the head and comb of a pheasant and the plumes of a peacock. The Fêng Hwang is a bringer of good luck and will not do anything to harm any living thing; it will not even eat grass. Its sweet song can sometimes be heard accompanied by the voices of many other birds, and the Fêng Hwang will also sing if anyone in its proximity is playing the flute.

FENRIR

In the mythology of the Scandinavian people, Fenrir or Fenriswulf was one of the evil monsters that participated in 'The Ragnarok', the battle that caused the end of the world. Nearly everything that we know about the mythology of these Northern people comes from two Icelandic texts, the 'Verse Edda' and the 'Prose Edda'. The Prose Edda was compiled in the 13th century by an Icelandic historian named Snorri Sturluson who recounted the story of the wolf Fenrir, the son of the mischief-making God Loki, and the brother of both Midgard's Worm and Death.

The Wolf caused so much trouble that the High Gods decided to shackle him to a rock in the Underworld. This was a difficult feat, for Fenrir was so huge that his jaws stretched from Heaven to Earth. The great beast easily broke the first two bonds with which the Gods tried to hold him, but the third was different. It had been created by a dwarf from the Land of the Dark Elves and was forged from the

Wooden carving of Odin caught in the jaws of Fenrir.

Wolves swallowing the old Sky Father, the forerunner of Odin, who was swallowed by Fenrir. Purse top decoration from the Royal Cemetery at Sutton Hoo in England.

noise of a cat's footstep, a woman's beard, the roots of a mountain, the breath of a fish, the nerves of a bear and a bird's spittle. Fenrir refused to be bound with this rope unless one of the Gods put his hand between his jaws. Tyr agreed and put his hand in position. The rope held and the God lost his hand, but Fenrir was held firmly.

Eventually the great terror of the Ragnarok came, heralded by a great winter that lasted three years. Fenrir snapped the bonds that anchored him and advanced to war against the Gods. Night fell over the world as another wolf called Skoll captured and devoured the Sun. Fenrir and the other evil entities Loki, Garm (the Hound of Hell) and Midgard's Worm battled against the Gods. Fenrir swallowed the mighty God Odin, all the other High Gods perished and fire consumed the Earth. However there was a small ray of hope left after this holocaust because some of the younger sons of the Gods survived. Odin's son Vidar slew Fenrir by tearing the creature apart, Earth revived and a new cycle of life began.

Nordic mythology surmises that it is only possible to bring about order by temporarily binding the chaotic and destructive powers of evil. Fenrir appears in the myths as the symbol of these forces.

FIREDRAKE

See also Dragon

In Northern mythology, Firedrakes were cave dwelling dragons. They guarded hoards of gold and other valuables that were hidden either in caves or in grave mounds. Because of its association with graves, the Firedrake was believed to be the spirit of the person buried in the mound and, in time, it became a symbol of triumph over death. The word 'Drake' here is derived from 'drakon', the Greek name for a Dragon, and has no connection with the aquatic bird of the same name. The Dragon was associated, in people's minds, with elemental forces like storms and atmospheric conditions and in Scotland strange lights in the sky were called 'Fiery Drakes'.

FOX

In the Middle Ages the Fox was a common symbol for the devil as it was considered to be a wily animal that was capable of expressing base attitudes. In Greek mythology, the Teumessian Vixen was a gigantic fox who ravaged the land of Cadmeia demanding the monthly sacrifice of a child to keep her from creating greater destruction. She bore a

A dragon of the Firedrake type. From an inn sign.

The Fox Goddess and a fox spirit. From a print by Kuniyoshi.

charmed life for it was fated that she could never be caught. She was chased by Laelaps, who had orders to kill her, and he was also divinely fated to catch whatever he pursued. To settle this apparently unsolvable problem, Zeus changed both to stone.

The Japanese Fox Spirit or Goblin Fox is also an astute creature and one who leads a nocturnal and shadowy existence. It is an uncanny, wary and sceptical spirit who can cause a great deal of mischief and is a master of illusion, causing mortals to see fairytale castles where there is only a pile of rubbish. The Fox Spirit uses its ability to create illusion to assume the appearance of a human being, usually that of a beautiful woman or a Buddhist monk. When it is metamorphosed into human form, it can be recognized by a flickering flame that appears over the head of the simulacrum, or by its reflection in water which shows only the shape of a fox. Although a Fox Spirit can be physically killed when it is changed into human form, it can never be spiritually annihilated. When it reaches a thousand years of age it becomes white or golden and sprouts nine tails. Then the Spirit troubles humans no more, for it ascends to Heaven where its magical powers reach their zenith. While it is still earthbound, the Fox Spirit is not always mischievous for, if it is well treated, it can bring good fortune.

The fox is also a rice spirit and the Goddess Inari, the Fox Goddess, is worshipped in order to make the crops grow. In China, the Fox Spirit is worshipped as "Great Father Hu" who is capable of making the elixir of life which he breathes out as a ball of fire.

FU-HSI

See also Cecrops

Fu-Hsi was the ruler of the mythical third age of China (2852-2738 BC). His shape was like that of the Greek King Cecrops, for he had a human head and a serpent's body. Sometimes he was represented with the head of an ox with horn-like growths on his forehead. Nu Kua was the consort of Fu-hsi and she, too, had the tail of a serpent. They are portrayed with their tails entwined in a fourfold pattern symbolizing the intermingling of their energies. He holds a compass and she a plumb line and a set square – measuring implements to create order out of chaos – and to give symmetry to a complex material environment. They taught mankind the art of writing, fishing and the domestication of animals.

Shen Nung, another Chinese ruler, was also represented with the head of an ox, but was otherwise human. He taught his people the uses of agriculture and agricultural tools.

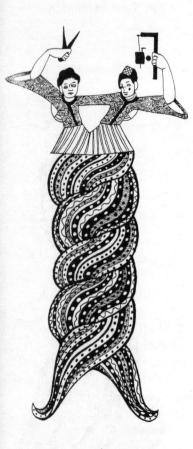

Fu Hsi and Nu Kua measuring 'the squareness of the Earth'. From a Chinese painting.

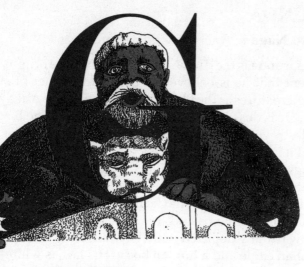

A bicorporate Gargoyle. From St. Mark's Cathedral, Venice.

GARGOYLE

The word Gargoyle is derived from 'La Gargouille' – the name of an immense dragon who lived in the river Seine at Rouen. The word Gargouille comes from the word for a throat, and gargle is derived from the same source. La Gargouille was able to make great water-spouts appear which caused devastation to all the surrounding countryside. The dragon's violent actions attracted the anger of St. Romain, the archbishop of Rouen, who was able to destroy the monster and burnt its remains in the market place. Up until the eighteenth century, the victory of the Archbishop was celebrated with a religious procession on 'Rogation Day' when an effigy of the dragon was carried around the town. Portraits of St. Romain often show him with a dragon at his feet or with his stole wrapped around a dragon or gargoyle; he is invoked against death by drowning. It is thought that the battle between St. Romain and this particular dragon symbolized the successful mastery, by the ecclesiastical community, over the flood waters caused by the Seine's inundations.

A Gargoyle is a carving often in the form of a head or, more rarely, the full body of a fabulous creature which projects from the gutter of a building to carry water clear of the wall. These strange, impressive and sometimes sinister looking carvings can be seen to have ambivalent meanings. They can be viewed as the symbols of the pagan gods of an older religion fleeing from the church, or as images of the demonical, monster-infested underworld (where they are held captive under the sway of a superior spirituality) frightening away the powers of evil.

Grotesque carved spouts are no invention of the medieval church, however, for many have been found in earlier periods. For example, a marble grotesque in the form of a lion's head can be seen in Athens National Museum dating from the 5th century BC.

Previous page
A Gargoyle with leonine
features. From the Grand
Place, Brussels.

The boar of the God Frey
was worn on a warrior's
helmet as a protective
talisman.

GARUNDA
See also Nāgā

The Garunda is the divine bird of India whose origins are so ancient that he is believed to be the forefather of such fabulous creatures as the Phoenix, the Simurg, the Anka and the Roc. He is described in the Mahabharata as "The Bird of Life ...destroyer of all, creator of all". He is a symbol of the Sun and it is said of this great sky bird that the Sun rode on his wings. In India, cosmic pillars which represent the ascendancy of light over darkness, often have a sculpture of a Garunda bird on the top. The Garunda was once completely bird-like but as time passed, his appearance changed and he is now usually depicted with the head, wings, beak, and claws of an eagle and a human body. His face is white, his wings are red, and his body is golden. This powerful bird was the steed and servant of the God Vishnu.

In legend, Garunda was the son of the Hindu sage Kasyapa. Vinata, his mother, took five hundred years to hatch him from a giant egg. She loathed her sister, Kasyapa's second wife Kadru, Queen of the Serpents. The rivalry between the two caused hatred between their offspring, Garunda, and the race of N 50⁻agā serpents. Garunda sought out and devoured one of these serpents daily until the Nāgās were in danger of extinction. A Buddhist Prince came to Garunda and offered himself in exchange for the Nāgās. The great bird was so touched by the offer that he became converted to the Buddhist doctrine Ahimsa or non-violence towards all living creatures and, in repentance, brought back to life all the serpents that he had killed. But people who are bitten by serpents still believe that only Garunda can help them.

Symbolically the conflict between the high soaring bird and the chthonian serpent, ending with the Garunda killing the Nāgā, represented the victory of benign, fruitful powers over the forces of drought and barrenness.

GOLDBRISTLES

Goldbristles (Gullinbursti), also known as 'the one with the terrible tusks', was a boar who belonged to the Norse God Frey and was considered to be one of the chief treasures of the Gods of the North. Goldbristles was no ordinary animal but a living example of gleaming metalwork created in the forge of skillful dwarfs. They made this great boar by throwing a pigskin into the fiery heat of a furnace and, by means of their magical powers, were able to draw out a golden boar whose mane and bristles glowed so much that,

even on the darkest night, the surrounding countryside was illuminated. He had the power to travel over land, sea and air; and drew the chariot of his master Frey.

Snorri Sturluson, the Icelandic author of 'Prose Edda', relates that Frey rode to Balder's funeral in his carriage drawn by Goldbristles. The boar of Frey was used as a protective symbol on the armour of soldiers going into battle, placing them under the God's protection. Goldbristles was also associated with Frey's twin sister Freya, a fertility Goddess whose nickname 'Syr' means sow.

The Norse Gods also possessed two more fabulous boars, one was called Battleswine (Hildisuin) and the other was killed and eaten every day by dead heroes in Valhalla. This boar, who came alive after being eaten only to be killed again, was called Sachrimnir.

An oriental painting of Vishnu and Lakshmi riding on Garunda.

GORGON

Myths in which the Gorgons or Gorgos figure can be found in 'The Metamorphosis of Ovid', Lucan's 'Pharsala' and Apollodorus's 'Library of Mythology'. In the best known versions of the myth, the Gorgons were three beautiful sisters named Stheno, Eurale and Medusa. They were the daughters of Ceto and Phorcys, the intrepid Old Man of the Sea. The Sea God Poseidon desired the lovely Medusa and, disguised as a horse, lay with her in a temple dedicated to the Goddess Athene. The Goddess was furious that they had desecrated her temple in this fashion and changed Medusa into a fearsome, winged monster. Instead of teeth, she had the tusks of a wild boar, her hands turned into brazen claws, her tongue protruded, her wavy hair changed into serpents and her staring eyes had the power to turn men into stone.

It is not certain whether Athene also transformed Medusa's two sisters but in Hesiod's poem 'The Shield of Hercules' these two Gorgons were "not to be approached and not to be described". On their belts were two writhing serpents and over the terrible heads of these Gorgons a great Dread quivered. These two sisters were immortal; only Medusa could die.

The hero Perseus swore a vow to King Polydectes that he would obtain the head of Medusa for the King. Athene, still seeking revenge, decided to aid Perseus by helping him obtain a pair of winged sandals, a helmet of invisibility and a pouch in which he could carry the Gorgon's head. Hermes presented the hero with a moon-shaped sickle called a harpe and Athene gave him a burnished mirror.

Perseus flew westwards, carried aloft by his winged sandals, to the land of the Hyperboreans where the Gorgons lay sleeping surrounded by the petrified shapes of men and beasts. Perseus, looking only at the reflected image of Medusa in the mirror, struck off her head with a single blow of his harpe. From out of Medusa's decapitated body sprung the winged horse Pegasus and the warrior Chysaor of Geryon. These were the offspring of Medusa and the God Poseidon. Perseus placed Medusa's head in his pouch and made good his escape from Medusa's enraged sisters by wearing the helmet of invisibility.

While Perseus was returning across the desert wastes of Libya, drops of blood fell onto the ground from the severed head of Medusa. Mother Earth received these drops and transformed them into venomous serpents of various kinds which is one explanation as to why that particular desert is so infested with snakes. Athene and the healer Aesculapius divided the Gorgon's blood between them. Aesculapius took the blood from her right vein which restored life, and Athene collected the blood from her left vein which brought death and earned for herself the title of 'Instigator of Wars'. Perseus later gave Medusa's head to Athene who fixed it

A classical Gorgon's head.

upon her Aegis. The Medusa shield of Athene was a favourite theme for armourers and sculptors in ancient times and also in the Renaissance.

Originally Medusa was depicted as a horse with wings, later as a woman with equine hindquarters and in early pictures she had wings on her hair which were eventually transformed into snakes. It has been suggested that the terrifying face of the Gorgon was derived from Anatolian and Syrian sculptures of attendant lions which had open mouths and lolling tongues.

Robert Graves, in his book "The White Goddess" considers that the gorgoneion or gorgon face was a mask worn by priestesses on ceremonial occasions to scare away trespassers. The priestesses would also hiss like snakes at an intruder which could account for the description of the snaky hair.

In ancient Greece, oven and kiln doors were similarly embellished with Gorgon masks to frighten away children who could ruin the baking and also hurt themselves by opening these doors. According to Frobenius, the Gorgon is a sign of the fusion of opposites; for example: beauty and horror. It is a symbol of conditions that are beyond the endurance of the conscious mind and will destroy whoever contemplates it. The Gorgon is also a sigil of the Great Mother Goddess in her most terrible aspect.

A spider from a Cherokee sun disc.

GRANDMOTHER SPIDER

In mythology, the Spider is usually feminine and harmless, but an object of fear and superstition. Victor Hugo said of the Spider that it was negatively determined, hidden in darkness, nimble, fierce and greedy.

Grandmother Spider was an important personage in American Red Indian mythology. She was the 'Grandmother of the Earth' and comforter of all living things, trying always to direct men's thoughts and destinies through her kindness and wise advice. But there was a hand of steel behind her velvet glove, for those who would not heed her words were lured to their death in the Underworld.

She was described as a bent, little old woman who was capable of transforming herself into a young and beautiful girl or into a spider spinning her web. She was rarely seen and spoke in a tiny voice hiding herself in the grass. But her two grandsons were not so reserved for they were the half-boy 'Twins of War'.

When there was only darkness, Grandmother Spider helped all the creatures of the Earth by stealing a piece of

The Gorgon with Pegasus. From archaic Greek carvings.

the Sun and thus gave light to the World. For some American Indian tribes, Grandmother Spider was actually the sun and in another American Indian myth, the sun was drawn up from the underworld in Grandmother Spider's web. Even to this day, the Red Indians say that a spider's web is shaped like a sun disc and its rays.

The spider sitting in its web represents the symbolic centre of the World and also has an affinity with the moon. In fact, in many myths, the moon is depicted as a giant spider.

GRIFFON

The Griffon, also known as a Gryphon, Yfrit or Griffin is a very ancient fabulous beast. Its origins can be traced back to the Near East where it appears on seal impressions. It was known in Egypt before 3300 BC and it is possibly more ancient than even these sources. Paintings in which this composite bird appears were popular in the Minoan and Mycenaean Empires.

In appearance, the Griffon had the foreparts of an eagle, the rear, tail and hindlegs of a lion, and its eagle-like head had pointed, upstanding ears like those of an ass. Feathers grew upon its head, neck and chest and the rest of the Griffon's body was covered in leonine fur subtly coloured in shades of tawny brown. Aelian said that the wings of

A Griffon. From 'The Triumphal Procession of Emperor Maximillian'.

Griffons were white and their necks were variegated in colour with blue feathers.

One of the most complete descriptions of the Griffon occurs in 'The Travels of Sir John Mandeville' Ch.85 :-

> *"In this land are many Gryffons, more than in any*
> *other place, and some say they have the body before*
> *as an eagle, and behinde as a lyon, and it is the*
> *trouth, for they may be so; but the Griffen hath a*
> *body greater than viii lyons stall worthier than a*
> *hundred egles. For certainly he wyl beare to his nest*
> *flying, a horse and a man upon his back, or two oxen*
> *yoked together as they go at plowgh, for he hath large*
> *nayles on his fete, as great as it were hornes of oxen,*
> *and of those they make cups there to drynke of, and*
> *of his rybes they make bowes to shoot with."*

A Griffon's head with pointed ears.

There are a number of different types of Griffon; the Snake-Griffon has a lion's body, a snake's head and a bird's hind legs, the Lion-Griffon is leonine but has hind legs shaped like those of a bird. These two types of Griffon were known in Babylonia and appeared in Hittite, Assyrian and Persian art. One Egyptian animal that corresponds to the Griffon is the Akhekhu, a four-legged, winged snake.

Herodotus of Halicarnassus, whose source was a poem by Aristeas, said that tales of Griffons came from the Issedonians, a race who lived beyond the Ural mountains. The Griffons were said to be guardians of hidden treasures in general and the vast gold mines of India and Scythia in particular. They were fearsome, greedy and rapacious animals; even their nests in the mountains were lined with gold. The Greeks called them 'Gryps', in Latin 'Gryphus' means to seize. The Arimaspians, a bold, one eyed race of humans, constantly tried to steal their treasures and eventually drove the Griffons away from the mountains.

Alexander the Great was reputed to have built a glass cage or a basket and harnessed it to six or eight Griffons. They carried him through the air and he was able to steer these unusual steeds by dangling a piece of liver on a spear in front of their beaks.

The blending of two solar creatures, the lion and the eagle shows that the Griffon is of a beneficient character. Symbolically Griffons represent the golden wealth of the Sun and these solar beasts drew the chariots of Jupiter, Apollo and Nemesis. The Griffon was particularly sacred to Nemesis as a bird of vengeance and was also considered to be a symbol of watchfulness.

The symbolism of the medieval Griffon was ambivalent. It could stand for the Devil but was usually an emblem of Christ. Christ is a lion because He reigns and is strong, an eagle because when He rises from the grave, He flies to Heaven. In heraldry, when the Griffon represents Christ, the colour of the eagle half of the beast is golden to signify divinity, and the lion part is flesh pink to signify Christ's human nature. Where the Griffon draws the car of the Christian Church, it symbolizes the union of divine and human in the Saviour.

GRYLLUS

A Gryllus. From a picture book by F. J. Bertuch.

The Gryllus, plural Grilli and also known as Stomach Faces, can be found engraved on Graeco Roman gems, on seal engravings and in the paintings of Hieronymus Bosch. A Gryllus is a distorted being whose body is of secondary importance to its head. Sometimes the body consists of two or more heads joined together, but often the body is left out altogether and the head is placed directly onto the legs. Some of the basic elements to be found in these drawings and engravings are the human face and lower body, female breasts, goat's heads, stag's antlers, bird's heads and the wings of birds, butterflies and bats.

It probably partakes of the same symbolism as the grotesque which is a general symbol for the world of phenomena.

GULON

A Gulon pressing itself between two trees.

The Gulon, known also as the Jerff, is described in Olaus Magnus' 'Compendious History of the Goths, Swedes and Vandals' where its habitat was the snowfields of Scandinavia. It had a brownish mottled fur that was much prized in hat-making, a hairy body, sharp claws, a bushy tail and a prodigious appetite. This obnoxious animal was said to be a cross between a lioness and a hyena and had the hyena's uncouth habits of eating dead, putrid bodies. Its stomach swelled so much as a result of its edacity, that it would find two trees growing close together, wedge itself between them and push the meat through its body.

The Gulon was hunted for its skin only, for its flesh could not be eaten. However, its blood was mixed with honey and drunk at weddings. It is one of the symbols of gluttony. Aldrovandus called it 'Gulo the Glutton'.

The Hai Riyo. A design from Japan.

HAI RIYO

The idea of the transformation of a dragon into a bird is common to both China and Japan. The Hai Riyo, also known as Tobi Tatsu or Schachi Hoko, is one of these composite creatures that comes from Japan. It is a cross between a bird and a dragon and has a dragon's head, feathered wings and a bird's claws. It may represent the Japanese rendering of the Chinese Ying Lung, the Winged or Proper Conduct Dragon, which is the only Chinese dragon that is portrayed with wings. Like all oriental dragons, it is an airy sign of clouds and rain.

HALCYON

The Halcyon, sometimes called the Altion or Alcyone, was named after Alcyone, Queen of Trachis, whose story is told in 'The Metamorphosis of Ovid'. Alcyone, the daughter of Aeolus the God of the Wind, dearly loved her husband Ceyx, the son of Lucifer, and was heartbroken when she heard that her partner had been drowned at sea.

As she stood looking sorrowfully out over the water, she descried far off a body drifting in to the shore. The corpse washed nearer and the grief-stricken Queen recognized the dead features of her own husband. In her despair, Alcyone leapt from an adjoining breakwater intending to join Ceyx in his watery tomb. But she found herself hovering above the water, changed into a small bird with a long neck, bright blue in colour with touches of purple and white in her plumage akin to that of a kingfisher. A sobbing lament came from

her slender beak as she flew to her husband's body and embraced it with her wings. This attracted the attention of some Gods who pitied her so much that they changed him also into a living bird.

Although metamorphosed into birds, the pair's love did not change and every year they mated and became parents. In the middle of winter, when the seas were rough and the winds boisterous, these birds collected the thorns of the Sea Needle and built a nest of them. This nest floated upon the waves on the surface of the sea. The female laid her eggs in it and brooded over them with her wings outstretched, while the male held back the waves. Aeolus kept guard over the winds, softening the breezes, and the seas became calm. For seven days before the Winter Solstice the waters were tranquil while the chicks hatched, and also for the seven following days when she fed her young; these days are known as 'Halcyon Days' and sailors may take these calm days for granted.

HANUMAN

Hanuman. From a frieze of monkeys and Hindu gods.

Hanuman was the leader of the monkey people whose exploits are recorded in the Indian epic 'Rāmāyana'. He had a monkey's head, a human body, a long tail, and is often portrayed with multiple arms; he had the heart and courage of a God and achieved eternal life by inveigling his way into Heaven and stealing some of the peaches of immortality. He lived a celibate life, and because of this, a wand that he carried was invested with magical powers.

In the 'Rāmāyana'; he assisted Rama (an incarnation of Vishnu) in the rescue of the God's wife Sita who had been kidnapped by the demonic Ravana, the multi-headed god of chaos and death. Hanuman helped defeat Ravana by leaping high into the mountains to obtain a great quantity of healing herbs with which to succour Rama's army.

Hanuman was noted for his speed, bravery and strength, and personified the animal aspects of the human personality, showing both friendly gaiety and destructive impulses. The monkey is said to symbolize the forces of unconscious activity which can be both dangerous and degenerating, but helpful when least expected. In China the monkey is a symbol of good health and success; in the literature of China, an animal that is akin to Hanuman is called simply 'Monkey'.

HARE

The Hare has been associated with the moon in the mythology of many countries. In China, it is a creature of augury and is known as Precious Hare, Hare of Jade or The Physician. One legend tells how a hare offered itself as a sacrifice by leaping into the Buddha's fire in order that He should have food. The Buddha, in gratitude, sent the hare's soul to the moon where, even now, it mixes the herbs that make up the elixir of life. The Hare in the moon is one of the symbols of resurrection. In China, the Lunar Hare is associated with Gwatten, the Moon Goddess and is said to derive its origin from the vital essence of the moon. Some Chinese paintings depict Ch'ang O, the Moon Queen, stealing the pill of immortality and flying to the moon with it accompanied by the white Hare who, according to Taoists, was the Queen's servant.

The Moon Goddess Gwatten. A Japanese painting by Takuma Shoga. 1191 AD.

In Europe, in the 'Zoological Mythology' of Angelo de Gubernatis, he states that :-

"The moon is the watcher of the sky, that is to say, she sleeps with her eyes open; so does the Hare ..."

The Hare is also believed to be a creature of the moon because of its fertility and its legendary ability to change its shape. The moon appears to alter its shape in the sky and is related to the cycle of female fertility.

As an extension of the idea of the Hare representing 'light in the darkness', the Manabozho or Manabush, the Great Hare and demi-urge of the North American Indians, stole fire from the sun to give to man. He was also their symbol of elemental existence and procreation.

In Greek literature and works of art, the figure of a Hare was used as a love symbol and was associated with Aphrodite, Cupid, and the Satyrs. It is difficult to say whether the love implied was physical or spiritual. It is more likely to have been the former.

Al-mi'raj, the Islamic Unicorn. It is a yellow hare with a single, black horn.

The Moon Rabbit can be compared to the Lunar Hare; the Aztecs believed that the moon was once as bright as the sun until the sun made it appear dull by throwing a rabbit onto its face.

HARPY

In Greek mythology, the three Harpies were associated with whirlwinds, storms, and sudden death. Homer thought that they were the personification of the storm winds and related that the Harpy Podarge mated with the Wind and gave birth to Xanthus and Balius, the two supernatural horses that belonged to Achilles. Although the Harpies were originally Wind Goddesses, they are usually regarded as the embodiment of guilt and punishment: two of the aspects of vice. In the 'Aeneid' they are described as vultures with women's faces and breasts, sharp curved claws and filthy underparts. They were always ravenous.

The name Harpy comes from the Greek 'harpazein' – to snatch or carry away, but modern philologists interpret one form of their name (Arepyiai) as tearers or slicers. They appear in the myths told about the journey of Jason and his Argonauts. When the Argonauts came to Salmydessus in Eastern Thrace, they found that two of the Harpies, Aellopus and Ocypete, were punishing the blind King Phineus for prophesying the future too accurately. Every time that a table was laid with food for the King and his retinue, the Harpies swooped down with shrill semi-human cries and snatched most of the feast. They infected the atmosphere with the fetid stench of their unpreened feathers and defiled the rest of the food with their foul excrement. Two of the Argonauts, Zetes and Calais, the winged sons of the North Wind, chased away the Harpies but were stopped from killing them by Iris, Hera's messenger. No one must kill these monsters for they are the executioners who carry out the sentences of the Gods from which there is no escape.

Part of the coat of arms of Nuremberg, Germany showing a Harpy and a double-headed eagle.

HIPPOCAMP

See also Nixie

The Hippocamp, known also as the Water Horse or Sea Horse, is a creature known both in mythology and in pictorial imagery in nearly every part of the world. It has been depicted in works by Iranian-Indian and Scythian artists, figured as the central motif of Roman mosaics, and formed the decorative element of many pieces of Baroque silverware. The Hippocamp is portrayed with the front half and forelegs of a horse co-joined to part of the body and tail of a fish. In heraldry the Sea Horse has webbed feet instead of hooves, a fin along its neck in place of a mane and is sometimes winged.

Hippocamps are the steeds of the sea gods and of night; they represent the humid element, lunar power, fertility and chaos. They drew the chariot of the Greek God Poseidon, controller of the sea, earthquakes and springs. He created the horse and is regarded as an equestrian deity. The blind forces of primordial chaos can be symbolized by the Hippocamps that are driven and controlled by Poseidon's trident. This trident has been identified by Charles Ploix in 'La Nature et les Dieux' as the magic wand used in water divining. Jung considered that the sea horses associated with Poseidon and Hades could symbolize sea foam and the rhythm of the waves.

Some types of the mythological sea horse are not composite creatures. The 13th century cosmographer Zakariyya al-Qaswini wrote in his treatise 'Wonders of Creation' :-

> *"The sea horse is like the horse of dry land, but its mane and its tail grow longer; its colour is more lustrous and its hooves are cleft like those of wild oxen, while its height is no less than the land horse's and slightly larger than the ass's."*

A Nereid riding a Hippocamp. From a Hellenistic silver bowl.

These superb creatures live in the sea, but will emerge to mate with any mare tethered near the water. Zakariyya al-Qaswini also stated that the resultant offspring of this mating were very beautiful; one foal of this cross-breeding was said to be dark with white spots like pieces of silver. Hippocamps who live in lakes and fresh water are sometimes seen in a very sinister light as they are fearsome monsters that are kin to the Nixies. They are known as Afancs in Wales, Goborchinu are Irish Horse-heads, in Scotland they are called Kelpies or Highland Water Horses. Sir John Rhys, the Celtic folklorist, wrote that the Femori – legendary invaders of Ireland – were commonly associated with the Goborchinu which in turn are linked to the Afanc and the Highland Water Horse; Captain Lionel Leslie some years later succeeded in showing that Femori was another name for the Peiste or Worm, the early type of European Dragon.

In the Romanian 'Physiologus', Hippocamps are called Endrops. An Endrop is said to be a shape-changer and would entice a man onto its back only to drop its unwilling rider into the water if the name of Christ was called upon. The Boobrie was a Scottish monster, a horse who came out of a lake and changed into a monstrous bird. The Ech-Ushkya (Gaelic Each- visge, 'Water-horse') is a handsome horse or pony that stands by the waterside waiting for some unsuspecting person to catch and ride it. That is the last action that its dupe will take, however, for the Ech-Ushkya is impossible to dismount and the man-eating fiend will leave only a portion of its victim's body, floating on the water, to show what had happened to it.

A Hippocamp, based on a drawing in 'Complete Guide to Heraldry' by A.C.Fox Davis.

HIPPOGRYPH

This mythological creature is truly a hybrid beast as it is a cross between a mare and a Griffon and, as the Griffon is also a cross between a lion and an eagle, it can be conjectured that the Hippogryph is, indeed, a very rare creature. Its hind legs and body are those of a winged horse with the forepart, beak and claws of a Griffon. It is probably a solar symbol although it lives in mountainous country in the frozen wastes of the far north.

Aristo took Virgil's metaphor "to cross Griffons with horses" and used this blend of the favourable aspects of the Griffon and the winged horse as one of the protagonists in his poem 'Orlando Furioso'. First the 'spiritual mount' was the steed of the enchanter Atlantes and after he had been vanquished, it became the mount of Atlantes' foster son Rogero. Later, Astolpho, an English Prince, claimed the beast.

HOG FISH

This amphibian, also known as an Ambize, had the body of a fish, a face like that of an ox, and hands instead of fins. It was much sought after by Congolese fishermen as it was reputed to be nearly 500 pounds in weight and had the

A Hippogryph with the winged body of a horse, the forelegs and head of an eagle and a twisted tail resembling a lion's mane.

flavour of pork. The hog is one of the few animals that can live and multiply in nearly every country of the world. Maybe the fishermen were indulging in wishful thinking along the same lines in regard to the hog fish?

Another fish that is associated with the hog is the Sea Hog. This fabulous creature had a head like that of a hog with the body and tusks of a boar and four legs. Only the hind part of the body was fish-like.

HORNED SERPENT

See also Serpent, Dragon

The best pictorial example of the horned Serpent comes from the decorations on the great Celtic cauldron found at Gundestrup in Denmark. Here Cernunnos (the Horned God) is portrayed gravely meditating in a seated position surrounded by his cult animals. One of them, the Ram Headed Serpent is clasped in his left hand. This highly individual reptile, which has a ram's head on a large serpentine body, is the most impressive of all the Celtic cult animals. Anne Ross says of it in 'Celtic Pagan Britain' that, in many sculptures and carvings, its size is so large that the Celts must have considered it to be divine. Cernunnos is the lord of the underworld, commerce, wealth and fecundity. His serpent too is associated with the underworld, fertility and especially with wealth that can be found underground. It is also found in sculptures, accompanying the Celtic equivalent of the Roman God Mars when he is figured as a therapeutic deity rather than as a divine warrior.

Another horned snake that also refers to primordial and cosmic forces is the Egyptian horned snake hieroglyph, but

A spotted Sea Hog.

The Ram-headed Serpent. From the Danish Gundestrup cauldron.

two other well known horned serpents do not appear to be the subjects of this type of symbolism and are most often to be found in bestiaries. The Cerastes is a flexuous serpent with four horns, like those of a ram, on its head. It captures its victims by burying itself in the sand leaving only its horns exposed. Out of curiosity, other creatures approach close to these horns and the Cerastes or Hornworm is able to kill them with its poisonous fangs. The Guivre is another sinuous serpent, immense and powerful. Its head is horned and dragon-like and it lives in forests and wells; like its relation, the dragon, it likes to dwell near water.

HORSES OF THE SUN

See also Pegasus

In the mythological tales of many countries, the Horses of the Sun were the steeds of the Sun God who drove them daily, harnessed to his chariot, across the sky from east to west. In Indo-European mythology Sun Goddesses were also connected with horses and travel. Winged horses depict the sublimation of those symbolic qualities ascribed to the animal – fleetness and dynamic power. When a white or golden horse appears with the Sun God or Goddess, it

The Horses of the Sun. A decoration from a Greek vase.

represents solar energy and light as opposed to the horses of the sea, the Hippocamps, which symbolize the wind and waves, chaos and the night.

The chariots of the Sun Gods Helius, Apollo and Mythra were drawn by white horses as was that of the Iranian Ardvisura Anahita. In most mythologies there are four horses harnessed to the Sun's chariot; Ovid refers to these four horses as Pyrois, Eous, Acthon and Phlegon. In some myths only two horses are named, for example the Norse Sun Goddess Sol or Sunna drove the horses Alsvid (all-swift) and Arvaak (early awake); in India the beneficient Sun God Surya drove only one horse which was multiple-headed and wingless. Norse mythology also includes the horse Skinfaxi (shining mane) who brought daylight and illuminated the world with its shining mane for his master Dag, the God of the Bright Sky. The night horse was called Hrimfaxi (frosty mane).

A chariot harnessed to a Human-headed Horse. A gold coin of the Aulerii, 1st century AD.

In Greek mythology, Phaethon, the son of the Solar God Helius, was obsessed with the desire to drive his father's fine white horses. When at last Helius granted him permission, the boy was not strong enough to check the speed of the horses which his sisters had yoked up for him. The terrified youth was unable to keep them on a straight line, and at first drove them so high in the sky that everyone on earth shivered; then so close to the ground that forests ignited. Zeus had to kill Phaethon with a thunderbolt in order to prevent the world from being laid waste.

The oriental Celestial Horse was described as looking like a white dog with a black head. It could fly through the air on large fleshy wings.

HUMAN-HEADED BIRDS

See also Ba, Harpy, Siren and Zû

The combination of a bird, the symbol of the soul and swift flight, and the human head, denoting life force and wisdom, is found in both pictorial and manuscript form throughout the world. The Anga is a bird with a human face who sat on a throne situated in the Kaf mountains in the Middle East; the human-headed bird of Islam is known as a Bahri. The Zägh is the human-faced speaking crow described in Islamic poetry; it is sometimes identified with the Roc bird. In India and other parts of the East, a bird with a human head and arms is known as the Kinnara. These birds are regarded as the messengers and musicians of the Gods.

Two peacock-like birds with faces similar to men are

The Bird of Hermes. From 'Ripley Scrowle' by J. Standish. 16th century AD.

68

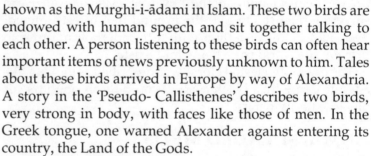

An oriental Human-headed Bird.

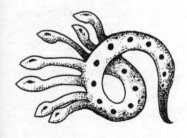

A Hydra. From a seal impression. Tell-Asmar 2500 BC.

known as the Murghi-i-ādami in Islam. These two birds are endowed with human speech and sit together talking to each other. A person listening to these birds can often hear important items of news previously unknown to him. Tales about these birds arrived in Europe by way of Alexandria. A story in the 'Pseudo- Callisthenes' describes two birds, very strong in body, with faces like those of men. In the Greek tongue, one warned Alexander against entering its country, the Land of the Gods.

The Bird of Hermes is a human-headed bird that can be seen in alchemical treatises where it represents the eternal cyclic nature of the Universe. This bird preys on itself (like the Pelican) by plucking out a feather every time it rises from the ground. The name 'Bird of Hermes' is derived from Hermetic philosophy, which is based on the writings of Hermes Trismegistus. The Bird of Hermes is shown with a bearded and crowned head.

HYDRA

See also Dragon, Jenny Haniver

One of the earliest representations of a multi-headed dragon known as a Hydra can be seen on a cylinder seal from Syria which dates back to the fourteenth century BC. It is part of one of the myths of the fertility God Baal which tells of his conquest over the seven-headed dragon Lotan (the Hebrew Leviathan), a creature identified with the watery forces of chaos and disorder. It shows the influence on both Hebrew and Canaanite mythology of the earlier Babylonian story about the slaying of the dragoness Tiãmat.

As its name implies, the Hydra is described in mythology as a personification of the fertilising powers of water. Even today, because of this association with fertility, anything that is hard to destroy either by its return to life or by reproducing itself, may be called hydra-headed.

In the description of Heracles fight with the Lernaean Hydra, the symbolism attached to its multiple heads and their powers of renewal are clearly shown. The Hydra's mother was the serpent maiden Echidne (she-viper) and her father was Typhon, a terrifying creature with a hundred dragon's heads sprouting from his shoulders and eyes which flashed searing flames. The Hydra was an unnerving sight for she inherited some of the most fearsome characteristics of each of her parents, being a powerful beast with a great dog-like body and eight or nine reptilian heads. One of these heads was immortal and was said to be made of gold. Heracles, the strongest and most fearless of all the Greek heroes, was rash enough to attempt to kill the Lernaean Hydra, a gruelling task set for him by his master King Eurystheus.

Heracles lured the Hydra from her lair beneath a plane tree at the seven-fold source of the river Anymone, and struck viciously at her serpentine heads with his club, but in vain, for as soon as one head was destroyed, two or three others grew in its place. Incensed by his inability to destroy the creature, the Hero shouted to his charioteer Iolus for assistance. Iolus hastily set part of the grove on fire, and seizing a burning brand, prevented the Hydra from growing new heads by charring the stumps of the heads as soon as they were removed. At last Heracles was able to sever the remaining immortal head of the Hydra and buried it still alive and hissing under a heavy rock by the roadside. The carcass he cut apart and dipped his weapons in the gall, making the least wound from any one of them fatal. Robert Graves, in his commentary to the Greek Myths, noted that the destruction of the Hydra seems to record the attempted suppression of the Lernaean fertility rites. But new priestesses, like the regenerated heads of the Hydra, constantly appeared in the temple on the banks of the river Anymone, until it was burned down.

A sculptural fountain of a Hydra. From Herculaneum, Italy.

The Bible too has its own Hydra and this "old serpent called the devil" is probably the best known dragon in history. The Apocalypse, the Book of the Revelations of St. John, describes not only this seven-headed dragon but also its battle with the great Archangel of the Light, St. Michael, who was eventually able to control his adversary.

"And there appeared another wonder in Heaven; and behold a great red dragon, having seven heads and ten horns and seven crowns upon his heads. And his tail drew the third part of the stars of Heaven, and did cast them to the earth; and the dragon stood before the woman which was ready to be delivered for to devour her child as soon as it was born. ...and there was war in Heaven; Michael and his angels fought against the dragon; and the dragon fought him and his angels. And prevailed not: neither was their place found anymore in Heaven. And the great dragon was cast out, that old serpent called the Devil, and Satan which deceiveth the whole world: he was cast out into the earth, and his angels were cast out with him."

This Hydra has been portrayed in many different ways. An etching by Durer shows the dragon as almost human in form; a tapestry from Angers in France, dating from the fourteenth century, depicts the Hydra as a seven-headed quadruped and the Hamburg Alterpiece of the Apocalypse figures the beast in its most typical form: as a seven-headed, two-legged Wyvern.

Left: A crowned Hydra. See also Apocalyptic Beasts.

Right: The Hydra/Dragon. A section of an altarpiece of the Apocalypse. 12th century AD.

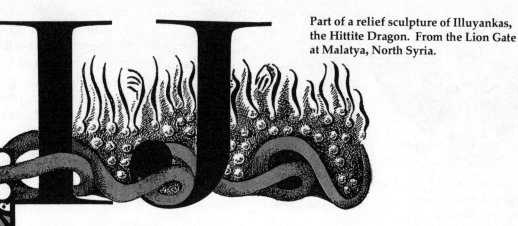

Part of a relief sculpture of Illuyankas, the Hittite Dragon. From the Lion Gate at Malatya, North Syria.

ILLUYANKAS

See also Dragon, Hydra

In some societies the Dragon, who represented the fertilising powers of the land, was ritually and symbolically slain in a ceremony designed to promote the fertility of the crops. The Hittite Purulli Festival was one of these fertility ceremonies which involved the recital or mime of the combat between the Weather God and the Dragon Illuyankas. A relief sculpture from the Hittite period shows Illuyankas with a coiled serpentine body. A number of erect subsidiary bodies are growing out of it. Presumably it was a seven-headed hydra, although the sculpture is in such a poor condition that it is now difficult to see the heads.

An old version of this story says that at first Illuyankas defeated the Weather God in a battle at Kiskilussa, but the God was not prepared to admit defeat and enlisted the help of the Goddess Inaras. She prepared a sumptuous banquet together with plenty of strong wines and invited Illuyankas and his family to partake of the feast. The Dragon and his family were delighted and all ate and drank until the palace was dry. As soon as Illuyankas was intoxicated, Inaras called her lover, Hupasiyas, to help her bind the Dragon securely with a rope. Inaras summoned the Weather God who came and slew Illuyankas and scattered his blood over the earth. The mime of this story would have been a piece of sympathetic magic designed to bring about the events that it represented, namely to revigorate the earth after the sterility of winter.

IMDUGUD

See also Human-headed birds, Zû

Representations of the Imdugud, the lion-headed bird from ancient Mesopotamia and Egypt, occur as far back as pre-dynastic times and even further. The bird with a lion's head and outstretched wings can be seen in early

72

Imdugud. From a silver
vase from Mesopotamia,
3rd. millennium BC.

A Jenny Haniver. From a
drawing by Aldrovandi in
'De Piscibus' 17th century.

inscriptions hovering above other animals ready to attack them. It is sometimes portrayed in relief sculptures tying the terrestrial and celestial deer together by their tails. In Sumeria it was the emblem of the God Ninurta-Ningirsu of Lagash and is also said to be the terrifying and death-dealing symbol of the fertility God Tammuz in his warrior aspect. In Akkadian mythology, its powers are transferred to Ningirsu's defeated foe: the human-headed bird Zû.

Later Mesopotamian seals show this creature with two birds' heads attached by the neck to its body instead of the head of a lion, to create a new visual type. The bird is likely to be the earliest form of the double-headed eagle.

JENNY HANIVER

It is relatively easy to make quite convincing fakes of small fabulous beasts like the Cockatrice and the Basilisk. So many of these fakes have been made, mainly in the 16th and 17th centuries, that there is a name for them. A fake of this type is known as a Jenny Haniver. It consists of the body of a real creature which ingenious manipulation has changed into the representation of a mythological beast. A Jenny Haniver is made by taking a dead ray or skate, distorting it by curling the side fins over the back, twisting the tail into a suitable position, drying, and then varnishing it. The resulting fake looks just like a fabulous creature, of the dragon type, with wings. Although not technically a Jenny Haniver, which is made with fish of the skate or ray tribe, other forms of faking have been carried out on the bodies of small animals. Wings have been attached to lizard's bodies to form Dragonets (little dragons). Fake mermaids were also constructed, mainly in China and Japan, by sewing together the top half of an ape and the tail end of a fish. These were so cunningly and carefully contrived that they looked real enough to attract collectors of rare and unusual items. One of the last examples that was on exhibition was to be seen at Barnum's Circus in America in 1842.

There was reputed to be a stuffed Hydra kept on the altar of a church in Prague which was carried off, in 1648, by Konigsmark and eventually came to Hamburg. In 1735, negotiations were carried out to sell it but before the deal was completed, a young man called Carl Linnaeus, soon to become the foremost genius of systematic botany and zoology in Europe, pronounced it to be a fake. Its heads, jaws, and feet were those of weasels, and snake-skins were glued on to the creature's body. Linnaeus presumed that it had been made by monks as a representation of the Dragon of the Apocalypse to deceive the credulous in former times.

The Kappa, a Japanese monster that is a cross between a monkey and a tortoise.

KAPPA

The Kappa is an aquatic Japanese monster which is said to be descended from the ghosts of people that have been drowned in the river where it lives. It has scaly limbs, webbed fingers and toes, the body of a tortoise and a monkey-like head with a cavity on top that contains a strengthening liquid. If anyone comes face to face with a Kappa, the safest thing to do is to bow to it, forcing the Kappa to respond in the same manner. Its strength-giving fluid spills, and the Kappa is unable to overcome and kill the human being, for men and animals are its natural prey. Another way to avoid the clutches of a Kappa is to throw a cucumber into its home waters. The cucumber is the Kappa's favourite food and it will spare the life of anyone who gives it such a treat.

This tale of a spectral animal is akin to popular fatalistic Japanese ghost stories but all is not completely doom-laden, for the symbolism of the monkey – the creature that the Kappa most resembles in intelligence – is ambivalent. It represents both base forces and unconscious powers. Here the unconscious forces can prove beneficial when least expected, for if a human could placate a Kappa, it would teach that person the art of restoring health by bone-setting which is its speciality.

KAR FISH

The prophet Zarathustra, who appeared in Persia in the early sixth century BC, saw himself as the messenger of Ahuramazda – Ormuzd, the Lord of Light. His teaching was that unity was a duality of the light (Ahuramazda) and of the shadow, death and destruction (Angra Mainyu) – which light was eventually destined to overcome. He hoped for the appearance of a saviour to herald a golden age for the righteous, one who would bequeath lasting torment for any man who turned to the destructive spirit Angra Mainyu and denied Truth.

In one Zoroastrian myth, the 'Guardians of the Light' were represented by the Kar Fish who protected the Tree of Life created by Ahuramazda. They circled the waters at the base of the tree and positioned themselves in such a way that, at any one time, one of their number could see Angra Mainyu. This evil spirit had assumed the shape of a lizard, which was also its symbol, in order to elude the watchful Kar Fish but it was difficult to escape detection for the fish had such keen eyesight that they could see a ripple on the water that was no thicker than a hair.

The guardian Kar Fish.

KRAKEN

See also Aspidochelone

The Kraken is another manifestation of the primordial enemies of the watery deep with whom combat is the supreme test. This ancient creature is one of the most celebrated of the marine monsters and was said to dwell in the sea off the shores of Scandinavia. In 1752, the Danish author Erik Pontoppidan, Bishop of Bergen, described the creature in his vast work 'The Natural History of Norway', a book similar to 'The History of Serpents' by Edward Topsell in that both were renowned for their generosity or gullibility towards traveller's tales.

He said that it was the largest and most surprising of all the animal creation and called it Krake or Kraxe – names probably derived from the crustacean crab. It had a smooth, round body that was one and a half miles in circumference with many arms or tentacles that encircled and crushed the strongest of ships, causing great loss of life. Human beings were said to be a great delicacy for the Kraken and, as it was able to eat without ceasing for months at a time, the seas near its habitat were particularly dangerous for shipping. The Kraken could also eject its waste products for long periods of time which may be the reason why amber is said to be one of its excretions.

The Kraken. From 'Historie naturelle des Mollusques' by Denys de Montefort.

When it lay dormant on the surface of the water, it resembled an island. The Bishop of Nindros is reputed to have once celebrated mass on its back and it made no movement at all throughout the ceremony, which was fortunate for the Bishop, as the Kraken was capable of creating a giant whirlpool when it submerged into the depths. Here the mythology surrounding the Kraken links it in a number of ways to the Aspidochelone.

Fishermen had mixed feelings about the Kraken for, although it was a fearsome creature, it was supposed to drive shoals of fish into their nets by lying on the ocean bed compelling the smaller fish to avoid it by swimming near the surface of the water. The fishermen concluded that when their catch was abundant, a Kraken was lying beneath them.

"Ye are mad, ye have taken
A slumbering Kraken
For firm land of the past." – Lowell, *Ode to France*, 1848.

From its description the Kraken seems to resemble a great octopus or squid, especially as it was reputed to be capable of turning the sea murky with a liquid that it discharged from its body, imitating the octopus's defensive 'ink-squirting' mechanism. Most portraits of it show an enormous squid with its serpentine tentacles entwined around the hull and masts of a ship. From Pontoppidan's description, a crab-like marine creature would be equally appropriate.

KUJATA

In Moslem cosmology the Kujata is described, in creation myths, as a bull-like animal with four thousand eyes, ears, nostrils, mouths and feet. The creature is so gigantic that, if a man were capable of living long enough, it would take him 500 years to travel from one eye to the next.

A serpent capable of swallowing up the whole Universe dwells in the Great Abyss, above the serpent is a layer of fire, above that air and then come the waters of the deep supporting the fish Bahamut. Kujata stands on the fish bearing a huge ruby rock on his back, upon which is an angel who carries the weight of the world.

Above:
Below:
Sea Monsters.

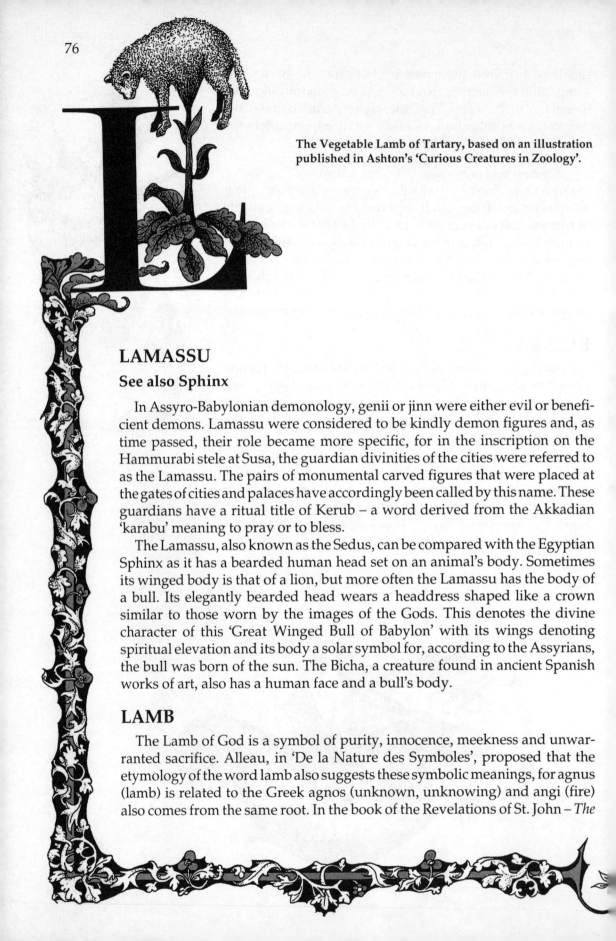

The Vegetable Lamb of Tartary, based on an illustration published in Ashton's 'Curious Creatures in Zoology'.

LAMASSU

See also Sphinx

In Assyro-Babylonian demonology, genii or jinn were either evil or beneficient demons. Lamassu were considered to be kindly demon figures and, as time passed, their role became more specific, for in the inscription on the Hammurabi stele at Susa, the guardian divinities of the cities were referred to as the Lamassu. The pairs of monumental carved figures that were placed at the gates of cities and palaces have accordingly been called by this name. These guardians have a ritual title of Kerub – a word derived from the Akkadian 'karabu' meaning to pray or to bless.

The Lamassu, also known as the Sedus, can be compared with the Egyptian Sphinx as it has a bearded human head set on an animal's body. Sometimes its winged body is that of a lion, but more often the Lamassu has the body of a bull. Its elegantly bearded head wears a headdress shaped like a crown similar to those worn by the images of the Gods. This denotes the divine character of this 'Great Winged Bull of Babylon' with its wings denoting spiritual elevation and its body a solar symbol for, according to the Assyrians, the bull was born of the sun. The Bicha, a creature found in ancient Spanish works of art, also has a human face and a bull's body.

LAMB

The Lamb of God is a symbol of purity, innocence, meekness and unwarranted sacrifice. Alleau, in 'De la Nature des Symboles', proposed that the etymology of the word lamb also suggests these symbolic meanings, for agnus (lamb) is related to the Greek agnos (unknown, unknowing) and angi (fire) also comes from the same root. In the book of the Revelations of St. John – *The*

Apocalypse – this Lamb is described as having seven eyes, showing that God's vision is all encompassing.

One of the traveller's tales ascribed to Sir John Mandeville in the fourteenth century features the Vegetable Lamb, also known as a Barometz or a Jeduah, which he said was a plant bearing a gourd-like fruit which split open when it was ripe, to disclose a little living lamb.

> *"And there growethe a maner of Fruyt, as though it*
> *were Gowrdes: and when thei ben rype men kutten*
> *hem ato, and men fynden with inne a lytylle Best, in*
> *Flesche, in Bon and Blode, as though it were a lytylle*
> *Lomb with outen Wolle"*

This story was derived from an earlier account by Friar Odoric of Friuli, who had journeyed to China in the first half of the fourteenth century, and who stated that the gourds not only grew in the mountains of Capsius but also on the shores of the Irish sea.

In the sixteenth century, more was added to the description of the Vegetable Lamb; it was complete in every detail with a very soft woollen fleece. It had blood but not animal flesh, for its flesh was like that found in a crab and its hooves were made of hair, not horn. The Lamb was connected to the plant by its navel cord and ate all the surrounding grasses that it could reach. When its food was exhausted,

The Lamb of God. From San Alemente de Tahull, Spain. 12th century AD.

An Assyrian Lamassu. From Dur Sharrukin. 721 -705 BC.

the cord withered and the Lamb died. Unfortunately for the Vegetable Lamb, its flesh was so succulent that it was the favourite food of wolves and other rapacious wild beasts.

The account of this little animal-like plant was once thought to be based upon a report of the description of the fern Polypodium Borametz which grows in hilly woods in China. However, it is more likely that it was a description of the cotton plant that gave rise to the story of the Vegetable Lamb – an account which had become so garbled by earlier writers that its original meaning had been lost.

LAMIA

See also Draconiopides, Tiāmat

In Greek mythology, the celebrated beauty Lamia was the paramour of the God Zeus. She bore him a number of children but nearly all of them were killed by Hera, the wife of Zeus, in a fit of jealousy. Lamia took her revenge by destroying the children of others and behaved in such a cruel manner that she was metamorphosed into a wild beast. She is usually portrayed with the head of a beautiful enchantress set upon an animal's body which has the claws of a cat on its front legs and cow's feet at the back.

Other ancient writings refer to Lamia as a creature who lived in a cave in the African desert. She was akin to the sirens for she could not speak; but her musical whistling lured travellers to her cave where she devoured them. This monster was a woman from the waist up and the rest of her body was serpentine.

Lamia is also supposed to have become one of the Empusae (Seccubus), vampires who lie with men in the night and

The beautiful but evil Lamia.

suck out their energy. One semi-human seccubus had the Assyrian name of Lilitu and was equated with Lilith, the first wife of Adam. In medieval occultism, Lilith is figured as the child-sacrificing demon Lamia and may originally have been a Libyan Goddess whose cult included infant sacrifice. The name Lamia is derived from 'Lamos' meaning an abyss which symbolizes depth and inferiority. Jung has stated that 'Lamia' is also the word for a huge and voracious fish, a creature that often figures as a denizen of the deep (Abyss), thus linking Lamia with early dragon deities like the Babylonian Tiāmat. The Goddess Hecate, a symbol of the 'Terrible Mother', the personification of the moon and the evil side of female nature, sometimes appeared in the form of a Lamia.

LEUCROTA

See also Crocotta

The Leucrota. From a medieval bestiary.

Caius Plinius Secundus (known as Pliny the elder) described Ethiopian Leucrotas in his 'Natural History' as the progeny of the mating of a hyena with an Indian antelope. This derivative of a hyena was a creature the size of a wild ass with the neck, tail and breast of a lion, the head of a horse and the legs and cloven hooves of a stag. It was reputed to be able to move extremely swiftly but was also handicapped, for it was unable to turn its head around to see anything behind because its backbone was rigid. Unless the creature swivelled around completely it would be blind in that direction.

The Leucrota could imitate the sound of the human voice, maybe in the same way as the hyena, by making a bark that sounds like hysterical laughter. It was commonly to be found in medieval bestiaries where it was described as the offspring of a lioness who had mated with a hyena. The Corocotta was also described in Bestiaries as a cross between a hyena and a lioness and could possibly be another name for the Leucrota.

Whatever their pedigree, all Leucrotas had mouths that split up as far as their ears and contained no gums. Instead, they had one long continuous bone in place of teeth at the top of the mouth, and the same at the bottom. These shut up like a box when not in use so that the edges of the bones could not get blunted.

The Leucrota is also known as the Leucrocuta and was confused, by Edward Topsell in his 'Historie of Foure-Footed Beastes', with a Manticore.

LEVIATHAN

The Biblical Leviathan or Lotan is the Great Fish of the Abyss, the primordial monster connected with cosmogonic sacrifice. It is also a symbol of chaos. It is easily identified with the Mesopotamian dragoness Tiãmat, for the Hebrew word for an abyss of waters (the Deep) is 'T'hom', a word often acknowledged to be a corruption of the name Tiãmat. Leviathan is the archetype of all things inferior and it is claimed that it was destined either for the supper of the Messiah or that on the Day of Judgement, the flesh of the Leviathan will be the food of the righteous.

> *"Thou breakest the heads of Leviathan in pieces and gavest him to be meat to the people inhabiting the wilderness". – Psalm 74.*

It is said that when the Leviathan is slain by the Archangel Gabriel, a tent will be made of its monstrous skin which will be so bright and shining that it is visible from one end of the world to the other.

Madame H. P. Blavatsky wrote that esoterically Leviathan represented 'the Deity in its double manifestation of good and evil' and that 'The Mystery of the Serpent of the Great Sea' was a term used in initiation ceremonies. The word Leviathan in Hebrew means approximately 'that which gathers itself into folds' or 'that which is drawing out' which suggests that the creature was serpentine in shape, while later Biblical imagery makes it a vast marine animal, possibly with whale or crocodile connections. There is a complete description of the Leviathan in the Book of Job, Chapter 41 :-

> *"Canst thou draw out leviathan with a hook? or his tongue with a cord which thou lettest down? Canst thou put an hook into his nose? or bore his jaw through with a thorn? ...who can open the doors of his face? his teeth are terrible round about. His scales are his pride, shut up together as with a close seal. One is so near to another, that no air can come between them. They are joined one to another, they stick together, that they cannot be sundered. By his neesings a light doth shine, and his eyes are like the eyelids of the morning. Out of his mouth go burning lamps, and sparks of fire leap out. Out of his nostrils goeth smoke, as out of a seething pot or cauldron. His breath kindleth coals, and a flame goeth out of his mouth. In his neck remaineth strength, and sorrow is turned into joy before him. The flakes of his*

Leviathan. From a 12th century AD MS.

flesh are joined together: they are firm in themselves;
they cannot be moved. His heart is as firm as a stone;
yea, as hard as a piece of the nether millstone. ...he be-
holdeth all high things: he is a king over all the child-
ren of pride."

LIGHTNING MONSTERS

In Zambia there is a belief that lightning is caused by an
animal who is lowered from above on the end of a strand of
a sturdy cobweb. This monster has the head and body of a
goat and the hindquarters of a crocodile. At the end of a
storm, it is hauled back to Heaven on its cobweb but if this
support breaks, and the creature falls to earth, it must be
found, killed and buried. The hunters of the Lightning
Monster must be protected with powerful magic for this is
a dangerous task. Aborigines of Northern Australia call a
similar reptile 'the Lightning Snake' and say that when it
raises its head to Heaven, it releases the much needed rain.

Haietlik. Wooden mask
from the Canadian
Northwest Coast Indians.

The Haietlik serpents of the North American Indians are
feathered reptiles who represent lightning. They are depicted on masks that are worn for ceremonial dances. These
masks often have small serpents rising out of the noses of
the larger figures and these too represent lightning. The
little serpents were the inspiration of an old Nitinat artist
who dreamed of a small lightning serpent that appeared
and danced on the nose of a larger Haietlik. These dance
masks have to be lightweight, as the performer, who per-
sonifies the lightning, has to twist and leap about for long
periods during the ceremonies.

LION

Leo the Lion is the image of the fifth sign of the Zodiac;
the Zodiacal Lion is ruled by the sun and signifies the
element fire. In Greek mythology, the Labours of Heracles
were equated with the progress of the sun through the
twelve signs of the Zodiac. The first labour of the hero, the
one that represented Leo, was to kill and flay the Nemean
Lion, a gigantic beast with a skin that was proof against
bronze, iron or stone. Heracles choked the lion to death with
his bare hands and wore its pelt as armour and its head as
a helmet.

In this myth Heracles took the role of a sacred king whose
ritual combat with a wild beast was part of the coronation
ceremonies in Babylonia, Greece and Asia Minor. Theoreti-
cally, by mastering the beast, Heracles obtained mastery

The Sun in Leo, a copy of
an interpretation from the
Middle East.

A Green Lion. From
'Rosarium philosophorum'
by Arnold of Villanova.
16th century AD.

The sacrificial cup of King
Gudea of Lagash. 2600 BC.

over the part of the year that the lion represented, the months of summer, and the wearing of the animal's pelt acknowledged this. The slaying of the lion by the sacred king shows the solar hero taming the searing heat of the sun.

In both ancient times and in the Christian era, the Zodiacal Lion of Leo is linked with the imagery of the tetramorph where it represents the fixed element of fire. The winged lion also belongs to the element of fire and symbolises solar light, morning, regal dignity and victory. In Christian iconography, it is the symbol of St. Mark as his gospel emphasises the royalty and majesty of Christ. The true lion of St. Mark (where it actually represents the saint) has a halo. In Hebrew mythology, the winged lion represents the south and the Lion of Judah.

The ancient science of alchemy conceals, in esoteric texts and enigmatic diagrams, attempts to penetrate the hidden reality behind all things; it is a system of cosmic symbolism. In alchemy the lion represents gold or the subterranean sun, solar powers and the element of earth. Where a Red Lion appears in a treatise, it corresponds to gold – the 'lion of metals', – sulphur, and the masculine principle. The Green Lion represents the young corn god before ripening into golden maturity; an illustration of a Green Lion would show the beginning of an alchemical work. The Green Lion represents matter in a raw green state out of which the principles of sulphur and mercury are extracted. The Green Lion disgorging the sun shows an alchemical drawing of the generation of wisdom (sun) through the formation of matter (lion). The 'blood of the Green Lion' in alchemical lore is the Hermetic Mercury which it vomits from its mouth together with the sun.

The Egyptian God of Sunrise and Sunset is shown as a lion with a head at each end of its body; the symbol of the Sumero-semantic solar and war god Ninib is a two-headed lion. The Sardula is a horned lion which can be seen portrayed in the Kesava Temple of Somnathpur in India.

LIONBIRD

See also Mušhuššu

The Lionbird is one of the symbols of the Mesopotamian God Nin-gish-zi-da, the Lord of the Good Tree – the God of Healing, in his chthonic aspect. It is an adjunct to the God's other symbol, a pair of copulating serpents, all of which can be seen on a sacrificial cup of King Gudea of Lagash 2600 BC. Heinrich Zimmer considered the complete design of the cup which consists of the serpents and two lionbirds, to be an early form of the caduceus, a wand with two snakes entwined around it surmounted by two small wings. In Greek mythology, the caduceus is carried by the God Mercury. The healer God Aesculapius carried a staff with a serpent wrapped around it as a symbol of his healing powers. Today the caduceus is still an emblem of the medical profession.

LUMINOUS BIRDS

Some bestiaries feature birds that have luminous feathers seen shining in the dark. The Ercinee are luminous birds which are named after the Hersynian Forest in Germany where they were born. Those that have seen the Ercinee, say that their feathers shine brightly and shed a phosphorescent glow on the ground to make safe the route that they are following. It is possible to trace that path by following the indicatory glow of their feathers. Aldrovandus noted that it was possible for a bird to become phosphorescent by sitting on a decaying nest, and owl's feathers have also been observed to glow after touching phosphorescent fungi that are found in rotting trees.

The Ercinee. From the Roxburgh Bestiary. 12th century AD.

The Lucidius is an Asian bird, sometimes called a Lumerpa, with a brilliant plumage that gives off light even after death, but if the feathers are plucked from the body, the light is extinguished. In one Bestiary, the Nightingale is called Lucina because she heralds the dawn of a new day in the same way that a lamp does.

LYNX

The Lynx is figured in the 12th century Roxburgh Bestiary where it is depicted as a type of wolf distinguished by spots on its back. However, some of its habits entitle it to be included in a book of fabulous beasts. For example, the urine of the Lynx is reputed to harden into a precious stone called a Ligurius. It is said that the Ligurius is the carbuncle, a ruby or a piece of amber, all of which are useful ornaments to mankind. The Lynx, aware of this, covers up its urine so that humans may not easily find it. Pliny agreed with this theory and also stated that the Lynx is only able to rear one cub in its lifetime.

The Lynx. From the Roxburgh Bestiary. 12th century AD.

The Lynx is sometimes called a Loup-cervier because of its abilities in the chase, and owing to its keen eyesight, (linx-eyed) it was reputed to be able to see through walls. In Christian symbolism it indicates the vigilance of Christ although it has been likened to the Devil because of its pointed ears and its penetrating eyes that gleam brightly when it hunts by night.

The Mafedet featured on a ceremonial animal palette from Egypt.

MAFEDET

This ancient Egyptian creature is portrayed twice on a votive palette from Hierakonpolis which, according to tradition, was the original home of the Kings of Egypt. Unlike the other animals depicted on the palette, which are treated in a naturalistic manner, the Mafedets are sculpted with unnaturally long and coiling serpentine necks, set onto the bodies of lions. Portraits of the snake-necked lion were found to have been made almost simultaneously in the earliest periods of both Mesopotamian and Egyptian art. It seems probable that pictorial representations of the Mafedet spread from Mesopotamia to Egypt.

MAKARA

See also Capricornus

The Makara is a fabulous monster that is depicted in many different ways. Its features usually include those of a crocodile, an elephant, a bird, a snake, or a fish, but whatever animals are included in its makeup, it always has some type of snout. Sometimes this snout resembles the trunk of an elephant, although it can be smaller like that of a crocodile or shaped like the horn of an antelope. The term 'Makara' is one that can be used for many composite creatures, but there must be elements of both mammals and fish present.

Makaras featured in older works of art have the forelegs and heads of elephants and are essentially Indian creatures, although they can also be seen in architectural carvings in Mayan and Aztec civilizations. An illustration of a modern interpretation of a Makara shows an elephant-headed bird with fish scales over its body similar to the elephant- headed birds that appear in the sculptures decorating a Nepalese temple of the seventeenth century. In Indian mythology, elephant-headed creatures with bird-like bodies are the mounts of the Lokapala – beings who hold the world aloft. One type of Makara has the upper half of an antelope and the lower half of a fish and is so similar to the goat fish symbol of the Babylonian Sea God Ea that it may have been derived from this source. The Makara was also linked by Madame Blavatsky to esoteric astrology. She said that the Makara should not be translated as a crocodile as it was rather the equivalent of the fish- tailed goat of Capricorn. She called it 'the Great Reptile of Typhon', and said that it seemed to be a debased symbol of the dragon of wisdom, the intelligent principle in humans.

The Makara, whose name means 'sea monster', is the steed of the river Goddess Ganga, and it is the mount of Varunda when he appears as 'God of the Deeps'. Marine monsters usually symbolize unfathomable depth, primordial chaos or divine power in manifestation.

A snake-necked monster from a medieval manuscript.

MANTICORE

The Manticore is also known as the Satyral, Manticora, Martikhora or Mantiserra. Pliny described the Manticora as:-

> "a blood red creature having the body of a lion, the face and ears of a human being with azure eyes set upon a long neck and a tail that ends in a sting like that of a scorpion. It can shoot out the quills of its tail like darts which can be spread all around for a great distance."

The mouth of a Manticore contains a triple row of teeth which fit alternately into each other and are vicious to behold. Its voice is shrill and resembles the combined sound of a flute and a trumpet, although it can also hiss like a serpent. The sturdy legs of the Manticore are so powerful that, when it leaps into the air, no place can contain it and no other creature can outpace the monster for it can run faster than any bird can fly.

The Manticore is one of the most dangerous beasts known to man for, not only is it impossible to capture, but it loves to eat human flesh. This is probably why its name, derived from the Persian, means 'maneater'. It has been likened to man-eating tigers and could be kin to were-tigers.

In Romanesque decorations, the Manticore is more often portrayed in the female form where she is covered in scales and wears a type of Phrygian cap. The female Manticore may be compared with sirens and other dangerous monsters, especially those connected with the primeval waters,

An elephant-headed Makara with the scales of a fish. From a modern Sinhalese motif.

A predatory female Manticore.

as scales on a creature of this type always allude to the ocean. She also appears in medieval Bestiaries as the symbol of the Prophet Jeremiah.

MELUSINE

See also Mermaid and Vouivre

Melusine. From an ancient woodcut.

In 1387 'Le Noble Hystoire de Luzignan', the story of Melusine or Melusina, the French Countess of Luzignan, was retold, from more ancient sources, by Jean d'Arras. She was reputed to be the daughter of the fairy Presina and the King of Scotland. When Melusine and her sisters sought to harm their father, Presina punished them. Melusine was transformed every Saturday into a monster. From the waist up she was still a beautiful woman but below she was a terrible serpent with silvery scales on her azure body. The curse on her also included the proviso that if her husband, the Count, ever saw her in her serpent form, she would become immortal and could never seek release in death.

She managed to keep her secret but, as all the children that she bore to the Count had deformities, he became suspicious and spied on his wife one Saturday while she was bathing. As soon as Melusine perceived that her husband had uncovered the secret of her terrible deformity, she shrieked three times, flew out of the window and disappeared.

Throughout the ages the immortal fairy serpent watched over her descendants from afar and, when disaster threatened any of them, she gave warning by screaming thrice. She also caused mysterious buildings to be erected overnight by workmen who vanished without trace in the morning. Unfortunately all these buildings had some defect in their construction. Melusine is the archetype of intuitive genius, intuition that is both creative and marvellous but is also maimed and malign. Sometimes Melusine is depicted with the tail of a fish instead of a serpentine body and is often winged. In fact she could be compared to a siren, a mermaid or a serpent woman like the awesome Echidne.

MERMAID

See also Merman

A Mermaid, a sketch of a lithograph by Eskimo artist Paulassie.

The Mermaid is one of the most ancient of all the fabulous creatures and one of the most popular. The image of a creature that was a beautiful woman from the waist up and a gleaming fish below, swimming powerfully through the sea, has inspired artists from all ages. Early portraits and sculptures of the Mermaid show her as a Goddess; in Syria she was the Goddess Dercerto and in Greece the Mermaid or Merrymaid was a disguise of the ancient sea Goddess Marian, known in that country as Aphrodite. It is here that she appears in her familiar form rising from the sea, carrying her attributes of a round mirror and a golden comb. The mirror is a symbol of truth while the comb, which can be likened to the fleshless spine of a fish, signifies burial.

The Sumerian goddess Nin-Mah, the Mother of the Universe and the essence or heart of the sea, was often portrayed as a Mermaid; it was written that her heartbeat governed the tides and waves of the Southern Ocean.

In Mesopotamian mythology, illustrations of the Goddess show that her fishtail was sometimes replaced by the lower half of a serpent and her son Ea also underwent the same metamorphosis. In esoteric tradition, Ea is often represented as a benevolent serpent. In contrast to the benign aspects of the male serpent, J. C. Cirlot considers that sirens, serpent fairies or mermaids may well be representations of the inferior forces in women with their beautiful upper bodies as the temptations that caused desires that their abnormal lower parts could never fulfill. Mermaids have reputations, like those of the Sirens, for luring men to their doom. Sailors, who are isolated from women by their careers and are thus particularly susceptible, say that they have seen them sitting on rocks at the site of such dangerous places as reefs and whirlpools, singing to themselves, coaxing the unwary to come closer.

The Mermaid has the ability to prophesy by foretelling the advent of catastrophes, tidal waves and storms; the wind is her song and in stormy weather she can be seen dancing on the waves. German and Scandinavian folklore relates that mermaids leave their seal robes on the seashore while they dance and, if the robe is found by a man, the owner cannot return to the sea but must stay with her captor until she can regain her robe. In Melanesia the same fate befell a porpoise girl who had left her tail on the beach. In time she regained it but warned her children, conceived by her captor, never to eat porpoise meat. Breton mermaids sing enchantingly as they comb their long hair and their great joy in life is to rescue young shipwrecked mariners and care for them. However, they are very possessive and will never let their charges leave them.

Misogynistic Christianity made her a symbol of the devil, but the greatest wish of a Mermaid is to possess a human soul. Only rarely can she achieve this, for only by transforming herself into an ariel spirit could a Mermaid win a soul,

This Mermaid from a 16th century AD bestiary, clearly shows links with the Melusine and the Siren.

providing she has caused no harm for 300 years.

The Mermaid, like the Merman, derives her name from the Anglo-Saxon word 'Mer' which means sea. In Denmark she is known as a Maremaid; in Japan she is a Ning Yo; in Ireland a Merdu. Pliny, writing in the first fifty years of the Christian era, called her a Nereid. She is also known as Atargatis (another name for the Goddess Dercerto), and as a Havfinë in Norway.

MERMAN

Some of the earliest depictions of Mermen were in the drawings of the Babylonian water God Oannes or Ea who was worshipped before 4000 BC. At first, pictures of the God showed a man- like creature wearing the head of a fish above his human visage and his legs subjoined to a fishtail. Later sculptured figures show a true Merman with the upper parts of a bearded man and the lower half the muscular tail of a fish. It was said that this God had a human voice and taught his people the arts of civilization. His retinue included both Mermen and Mermaids who held vases of lifegiving water.

The Greek hero Heracles wrestling with The Old Man of the Sea.

In Greek mythology, the Merman Proteus was the shepherd of the flocks of the ocean and is portrayed bearing a shepherd's crook. As flowing water is constantly changing, Proteus was also able to change his shape at will. Another Merman named Triton was the son of Poseidon, the Sea God, and Amphitrite, whose name means 'The Sea'. Triton was at first female but later became masculinized and became known as 'The Old Man of the Sea'. This amphibious being was very jealous of his skill at playing the conch shell trumpet, and drowned the trumpeter Misenus whose ability exceeded his own; but Triton was not always successful, for once Heracles wrestled with the sea god and overcame him. Later, he founded a tribe or school of Tritons. These Mermen had sharp teeth, hair made of seaweed, narrow hands like bi-valve shells, scaly bodies, fins on their breasts and bellies, and dolphin's tails. They were lascivious, but also benevolent and obliging. The earliest weathercocks placed on the top of tall buildings to indicate the direction of the wind, used to display a Triton. The cockerel was a later modification.

This Triton from a 16th century AD bestiary may show it in its earlier female form.

In medieval times Guillame Rondelet described in his 'Book of Sea Fishes' a type of merman called a Monk Fish that lived in the sea. The Monk Fish had a tonsured head, a scaly cowl and a robe that ended in a fish tail. It was known in China as the Hai Ho Shang (Sea Buddhist Priest). It was said to be so aggressive that it upturned junks and drowned the crew. It could only be driven away by the strong stench of burning feathers or by a member of the threatened crew performing a ritual dance. The Chinese believed that Mermen or other sea monsters with human heads were the spirits of drowned men desperate to find a human substitute to take their place.

The Bishop Fish, described in Gesner's 'Historia Animalium', had a mitred headdress, arm-like fins and heavy legs. Sightings of Mermen were reported in the Hebrides and were distinguishable from all other fish men by their colouring. These men from Minch were coloured blue from head to tail.

Monsters like Mermen and Mermaids that are born in the depths of the ocean, the abyss, are also considered to be symbols of sterility for salt water has the ability to destroy higher forms of land life.

The self destructive Mermecoleon.

MERMECOLEON

The quotation 'The old lion perisheth for lack of prey' – Job 1V II, in the Septuagint text of the Scripture, used the word Mermecoleon instead of lion. Mermecoleon is a name based on the word 'Myrmex', used by Aelian to describe an Arabian lion, a word so rarely used that it soon became forgotten. When the text was read in later years, the word 'Myrmex' in Greek meant an ant, so that a literal translation of the quotation would read, 'The old Ant Lion perisheth for lack of prey'.

This linguistic misunderstanding gave rise to a story about a fabulous creature called the Mermecoleon, Mirmecoleon or Ant Lion. The Mermecoleon is said to have been born when the seed of a lion fell onto the ground and impregnated some ant's eggs. This hybrid had the head of a lion and the hind parts of an ant and, as its father was a carnivore and its mother was a vegetarian, the creature had the characteristics of both. It was unable to eat meat because it was a vegetarian and was unable to eat grain because it was a carnivore. As a consequence of this, it soon starved itself to death.

MIDGARD'S WORM

See also Worm.

In many myths there stands, at the centre of the world, a pillar, pole or tree which acts as a support for the Earth. In Norse mythology this world support was the ash tree Yggdrasill. Among the Anglo-Saxons there was a strong belief that there were many worlds, said to be seven or nine, each supported by this high and stately tree. Its branches overhung these worlds and reached far into the heavens. The tree, in its turn, was supported aloft by three great roots: one root was under the protection of the Gods; another was cared for by the frost giants; under the third was a roaring cauldron with the dragon Nidhogg gnawing at the tree's roots from below. At the foot of the Yggdrasill tree sit the three Norns, Goddesses of Fate, passing the cosmic shuttle between them as they weave the fates of men. They represent the three faces of the Moon Goddess, waxing, waning and fullness.

The Earth at the centre of the tree was encircled by the World Serpent known to Norsemen as Midgard's or Jormungand's Worm. It created the oceans which it swallowed only to regurgitate them. This reptile was doomed to lie in the sea encircling the World with its tail in its mouth; should the tail ever be wrenched out, disaster would follow. In the Voluspa it is proclaimed that the deluge will commence when the serpent awakes to destroy the universe.

Midgard's Worm naturally presented a challenge to the red-headed, hot-tempered Weather God, Thor, who was

Midgard's Worm.

determined to smite the great Worm dead with his hammer, regardless of the consequences. Snorri Sturluson tells of the encounter in the 'Prose Edda' relating how Thor persuaded the giant Hymir to take him fishing and, using the bait of an Ox head, caught the Worm on his line. Hymir turned yellow with terror, grabbed his knife and hacked Thor's fishing rod overboard. The serpent sank down into the depths of the sea and Thor was so mortified that he up-ended Hymir into the water and waded ashore.

Eventually Thor and Midgard's Worm met again in a more deadly encounter and the World Serpent and Thor succeeded in slaughtering each other at the Ragnarok – the Doom of the Gods. Jung defines the worm as a libidinal figure which kills instead of giving life; he considers that its chthonic and base characteristics make it a symbol of death.

MINOTAUR

The Minotaur was the unnatural offspring of Pasiphaeë, wife of the King of Crete, and a white bull from the sea that had been withheld from sacrifice. The monster that was born from this union had a bull's head and a human body and was a creature that looked so appalling that King Minos, to conceal Pasiphaeë's disgrace and his own humiliation, hid mother and child in an inextricable maze called The Labyrinth. This maze was built for the King at Cnossus by the famous Athenian craftsman – Daedalus.

In requital for the death of one of his children, King Minos demanded tribute from the Athenians every nine years in the form of seven youths and seven maidens. These fourteen young people were destined to become the victims of the ferocious bull-man, Asterius the Minotaur. The hero Theseus so pitied these unfortunates, that he took the place of one of them and was also thrown within the labyrinth to meet his fate at the hands of Asterius. In the resulting battle Theseus managed to kill Asterius and, with the aid of a ball of thread given to him by Minos' daughter Ariadne, he managed to find his way out of the Labyrinth and fled from the country taking Ariadne with him.

Every myth which alludes to tributes, victorious heroes and monsters, usually illustrates a cosmic situation or a social implication in the form of a famine, oppression by a dictator or a similar disaster. The monster is the sign of the animal side of man's nature, while tributes and sacrifice indicate the sentiments and emotions of his finer side. The predominance of the spiritual side of man is symbolized by

The Norse tree Yggdrasill is encircled by Midgard's Worm.

Theseus fighting the Minotaur. From a piece of pottery.

the knight, and the prevalence of the monstrous by creatures like the Centaur or Lamassau with animal bodies. The inversion of this, an animal's head upon a human body shows the domination of the baser forces carried to the extreme conclusion. The Minotaur's dual nature, half man and half beast, implies the dominance of the savage passions of nature. Theseus' battle with the Minotaur at the heart of the Labyrinth, where man overcomes and thus unites with the beast of his hidden nature, makes him born again into a new state of completeness.

MUŠHUŠŠU

See also Tiāmat, Lionbird

Mušhuššu or Sirrush is the fire-red monster which is portrayed in relief sculpture on the Ishtar Gate – once an entrance to the city of Babylon. It was raised to the glory of the God Marduk by Nebuchadnezzar.

> *"I placed in the entrance way some proud bulls in*
> *bronze and angry dragons. I embellished the gate in*
> *this manner to gain the admiration of all people."*

It was the personal symbol of three gods; the hero Marduk who killed the dragoness Tiāmat and was god of both salt and fresh water, Nabu the son of Marduk who was the god of the written word, and Nin-gish-zi-da, the god of fertility and the waters of the abyss. As the attribute of these gods, Mušhuššu could also replace them and became itself the symbol of fertility caused by the presence of nourishing waters – the springs of learning. The Lionbird was also an attribute of Nin-gish-zi-da and could be consanguineous with Mušhuššu.

Mušhuššu. A drawing of the relief on the Ishtar Gate at Babylon.

Part of a stone relief of a Nāga. From India, 13th century.

NAGA

See also Garunda

Nāgās are the semi-divine, semi-human serpent spirits of Indian origin who are known throughout South East Asia and are so firmly established in the mythology of East Asia that, when the doctrines of Gautama Buddha were accepted in this area, the Nāgās were adopted by the new creed. The Nāgā King Mucilinda is reputed to have sheltered the meditating Buddha from chilling winds and rain for seven days by protecting the Lord with his hoods and coils. This is a favourite theme used by Asian artists when portraying the Buddha.

Nāgās, the females are known as Nāginis, are depicted in three different ways: completely serpentine, fully human but with serpents coming out of the back of the neck, and half human and half serpent with the upper half of a man or woman, crowned with a serpent hood, and the lower body of snake. The fully human shape of some Nāgās is assumed because some of the actions attributed to them can only be performed by an entity within a human form. Their natures are also threefold being animal, human, and divine.

These serpentine creatures are the symbols of water whether it is for good or for evil – the fertility of the land or the flood. They have the ability to create clouds and also have the power that enables them to open the floodgates of heaven. As Nāgās are the spirits of the life force of water, they are reputed to dwell in the waters of springs, in lakes and in rivers. They have magnificent jewel-encrusted palaces at the bottom of the sea.

Nāgās are the possessors of a great wealth of precious jewels, but their valuables do not give them complete satisfaction for they always strive to gain

A Nāgini stone relief from Gondwana, India.

a soul and immortality. When the gods and demons sought to 'churn the waters of the seas' in order to force the elixir of life to rise to the surface, the Nāgās were careful to place themselves in a position where they could lap up a few drops. Their success enabled them to command a limited immortality but, unfortunately, in their eagerness to obtain the coveted liquid they split their tongues on the spiky grass that covered the ground where the elixir fell. Ever since that time Nāgās have had forked tongues.

Mahayanists divide the Nāgās into four groups; divine Nāgās who produce the clouds and the rain, earthly Nāgās whose duty it is to make sure that all outlets are open and that rivers are running freely, hidden Nāgās who guard the treasures of the world, and heavenly Nāgās who, as 'Guardians of the Threshold' protect the heavenly palace and also the temples of many major and minor deities. Guardian Nāgās are often portrayed as coiled serpents with human heads who act as the guardians of esoteric knowledge by protecting the sacred pearl of divine wisdom at the centre of their labyrinth coils.

NIXIES
See also Hippocamp

The Nixies are Slavonic water spirits who are depicted as winged maidens with either a bird's legs or a fish tail. The male Nix are old and gnarled with slit ears, fox tails and hooves on their feet. These they endeavour to conceal in order not to scare away the young maidens whom they seek to waylay. The Nix is able to alter his appearance in order to capture young women and presents himself as a golden haired boy with a harp on which he plays enticing music. On other occasions, the Nix appears as a water-horse with a black shining coat, a white star on its forehead, a narrow snout and a flowing mane and tail. No girl should be fooled by him, however, for great harm will befall any woman who strays into the Nix's path as he will seduce and drown her.

Nixies are also found in England. One called Peg Powler was seen in the River Tees. She had green hair and an insatiable desire for human life. Jenny Greenteeth was a sprite who haunted the River Ribble and was associated with the green plants that grew on the water margin. She was an evil creature who claimed one life every seven years by dragging her victim down to drown in the river. Pictures of her show a creature with a human body, wings, a fish tail and bird's legs; these representations of Nixies show aspects in common with sirens and mermaids.

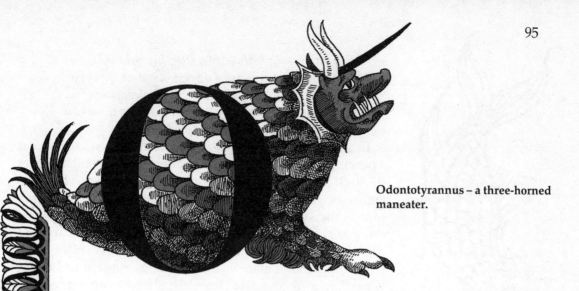

Odontotyrannus – a three-horned
maneater.

ODONTOTYRANNUS

An anonymous writer, now known as pseudo-Callisthenes, wrote a number of stories about Alexander the Great (356-323 BC) which mixed historical fact with legend. One of the characters of these Alexandrian romances was the amphibious Odontotyrannus. It lived in the River Ganges in India and was easily distinguished from other monsters in the river by the three horns on its head and its gigantic size. It was so huge that it could swallow an elephant in a single gulp and nothing would deter it from attacking people; neither weapons nor fire had any effect. Alexander was reported to have lost twenty six of his men in the maw of one of these monsters when they unwittingly went swimming in the river that it regarded as its own.

ORIENTAL DRAGON

See also Hai Ryo

The Dragon holds a remarkable position in China, for this country is the most dragon-orientated place in the world. Unlike Western Dragons who, since the advent of Christianity, are associated with evil, the Chinese Dragon is eminent in the affections of the Chinese people who praise its wonderful powers and venerate it as the symbol of wealth, wisdom and water. It is frequently represented in art or literature as humanity's benefactor, for it is the Dragon who causes the clouds to form and rain to fall. It could be as mild as gently falling rain or as savage as the greatest thunderstorm.

Wang Fu, during the Han dynasty, described the Chinese Dragon – the Lung – thus:-

The little Yu Lung – the carp dragon – is a symbol of success in examinations.

The Lung Wang, the dragon king who controls all storms.

"His horns resemble those of a stag, his head that of a camel, his eyes those of a demon, his neck that of a snake, his belly that of a clam, his scales those of a carp, his claws those of an eagle, his soles those of a tiger and his ears those of a cow."

In addition he has whiskers, a beard that is said to conceal a pearl, a voice like the jangling of copper pans and he hears through his horns as his ears are non-functional. There are eighty-one scales down a Dragon's back – nine times nine - nine is the symbol of Yang, the male principle. However, there are both male and female Dragons. Females are distinguished by straight noses, round manes and strong tails, while the horns of males are undulating, concave and steep. When Dragons copulate they change into small snakes and it was generally considered that Dragons hatch from eggs laid by these serpents.

Paintings of Chinese Dragons often show them reaching out for a pearl or round-shaped object. There is a great deal of controversy about the symbolism of this pearl. Among other suggestions, it is thought to represent the sun, the moon or thunder – all of which are associated with dragons and their control of the elements. Another theory is that this orb represents truth and life, two other aspects associated with Chinese dragons who are reputed to live for many centuries and are imbued with the wisdom to know the value of truth.

It is very difficult to classify Lung Dragons as there are so many different types of them. Most sources list the following: the T'ien Lung or Celestial Dragon is a Dragon that resembles the description given by Wang Fu. He guards and supports the temples of the Gods. The Shen-Lung or Spiritual Dragon is the one who controls the winds and the rain. This is reputed to be the five-toed Imperial Dragon whose shape only the Emperor was permitted to wear embroidered on his raiment. If anyone else was caught wearing an image of a Dragon with five toes on his clothing, he was punished by death. The Ti-Lung or Dragon of Earth holds the rivers and streams in its power. The Fu-ts'ang or Dragon of Hidden Treasures, guards the hidden wealth of the earth. Most Chinese dragons can fly without wings but the Ying Lung, the Winged or Proper Conduct Dragon, is the only one with wings. The Yellow Dragon is the Dragon Horse who appeared from the River Lo bearing the eight trigrams of the I Ching on its back. The Lung Wang, the Fire Dragon, or Dragon King, controls all storms and has a human body and a Dragon's head. He never dies and resembles the

The Shen Lung – the
spiritual dragon.
Embroidery from the robe
of an emperor.

Nāgās of India in the fact that he dwells in a fabulous palace
at the bottom of the sea. The Yü Lung or Fish Dragon is a
fish-shaped Dragon that was once a carp who succeeded in
leaping the waterfalls at Dragon's Gate and was metamorphosed into a Dragon. This Dragon is the symbol of success
in passing examinations. These are only some of the many
types of Dragon that include the Coiled Dragon, the Horn-
less Dragon and the Blue Dragon.

The Blue or Azure Dragon deserves a special mention for
it plays an important part in the system of Fêng Shui which
is a geomantic system prevalent throughout China before
Communism and still practised in other parts of the Orient.
There are two creatures involved in Fêng Shui: the Blue
Dragon and the White Tiger. As the Dragon is Yang, so also
are mountains, large rocks, steep waterfalls and ancient

A Japanese dragon. Part of a Ukiyo-ye triptych.

The Ying Lung – the proper conduct dragon. From an oriental culture chart.

pines. The White Tiger represents Yin, the female principle. Yin places are low-lying, valleys, and damp areas. A diviner of Fêng Shui will study the raised portions of the land – the veins of the Blue Dragon - in relation to the valleys, and note the auspicious places, those that are in harmony with a correct balance of Yin and Yang, which would be suitable for homes, offices and the sombre but important task of burying the dead.

China can be a parched land and it is to the dragon that the people looked to bring rain. In times of drought, it was the custom to lower the bones of a tiger into a 'Dragon Well' and leave them there for three days. The belief was that the Dragon and the tiger cannot meet without fighting and it only needs the Dragon to shift his position to allow the clouds to lift and the rain to fall. The tiger's bones were used to excite the Dragon and cause him to rise up, so ending the drought.

Another way that the Chinese seek to make rain is to make a large wood and paper dragon and carry it in procession. If no rain falls, the effigy is destroyed which, in theory, so enrages the Rain Dragons that they leap up and inadvertently release the clouds.

The Oriental Dragons and Serpents have the utmost cosmic significance for the Chinese. Chuang-tzu came to the conclusion that they are symbols for 'rhythmic life' and the Dragon has always been associated with lightning, rain and fecundity. The Japanese dragon, who is called a Tatsu and is similar to the Chinese dragons but more serpentine in shape, also has this symbolism but as Japan is not such an arid country as China, the Tatsu is more closely associated with the sea than with rain.

'Leoparde'. From the Oxburgh hangings that were derived from Conrad Gesner's 'Historia Animalium'.

PANTHER

The mythical Panther, also known as a Pard, Pardel, Panthera, Pardus or Pardalis, is described in Bestiaries as a handsome, parti- coloured, four-footed animal. It can easily be distinguished by its spotted coat which is coloured tawny, black and white. The Panthera that figured in 'The Travels of Sir John Mandeville' had a blood red skin which shone in the rays of the sun and was worth its weight in gold. In heraldry it has cloven hooves, the tail of a horse and the claws of an eagle instead of forefeet.

It is said that a Leo-pard born from the adultery of a lioness and a pard, is considered to be the Panther's inferior offspring. The Leopard, which is equated with Argus-of-the-thousand-eyes, has the same symbolism as the Panther. Both are symbols of ferocity and valour, expressing the aggression and strength of the lion without its solar significance. The Ounce can be considered to be the same creature as the Leopard.

Plutarch wrote that the name of Osiris, the Egyptian God of the Underworld, could have been interpreted as O = many, and Iri = eye. The 'many eyed Osiris', who was also known as The Watcher, was symbolized by the Panther or Leopard because the spots on the animal's skin resembled a multitude of eyes. In Egypt, the image of Osiris was sometimes depicted as a crouching leopard surmounted by an open eye and a spotted leopard skin was suspended near effigies of the God.

In Bestiaries and mystical allegories, Jesus Christ is described as a Panther. They state that when the Panther has eaten a meal, he sleeps for three days, and upon awakening, emits a sweet ringing sound and from his throat there comes a scent of such sweetness that none can resist it. All come to him except the serpent who hides in his hole in the ground for, in these allegories, the serpent is the Devil.

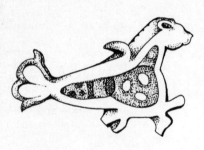

Previous page
The Sea-Panther or
Leopard. A Roman bronze
brooch from the Isles of
Scilly.

A Parandrus. From a 12th
century bestiary.

PARANDUS

This animal is often featured in medieval bestiaries where it is shown with ibex-like branching horns, cloven hooves, the head of a stag and a deep shaggy coat like that of a bear. When it is frightened, its coat changes colour so as to blend into the background, light against stone, green against bushes. It is said to be able to reflect the colour of all trees, shrubs and flowers or of any spots in which it is concealed. For that reason it is rarely captured.

PEGASUS

See also Hippogryph, Chimera and Gorgon

Pegasus was a winged horse born out of the union of the Gorgon Medusa with Poseidon, the Sea God, who visited her in the form of a stallion. Pegasus is a lunar animal, and is described as a white horse – the colour of the moon – with golden wings. It has also been noted that Pegasus is white because it represents one of the aspects of the Great Goddess when, as the Mare-headed Mother, she was known as Leucippe – the white mare.

The name Pegasus means 'of the springs of water' and this describes its ability to cause a fountain of water to gush out wherever it stamped its moon shaped hoof. In order to assist the Muses of Mount Helicon, Pegasus created a fountain, known as 'The Horse Well' for them at Hippocrene. The waters conferred poetical inspiration on all who drunk there.

The hero Bellerophron caught the magical horse by throwing a golden bridle, a present from the Goddess Athene, over Pegasus's head while the stallion was drinking at another of his fountains. This caused the wild horse to become tame and obedient. He willingly flew his master to the lair of the Chimera, an act which enabled Bellerophron to kill the monster, whereupon the hero was so elated by his success that he vaingloriously rode Pegasus aloft to Olympus. Zeus was furious at his presumption and sent a gadfly to sting Pegasus under his tail. Pegasus reared, flinging Bellerophron back to earth again, but completed his flight to Olympus where Zeus now uses him to carry his thunderbolts.

In the state religion of Rome, Pegasus was reputed to bear the Emperor on his back to the 'Land of the Dead' and images of Pegasus can be found on many Roman tombstones. The winged horse is symbolic of the combination of higher and lower natures and the striving to achieve the higher with the innate capacity for inverting evil into good.

Pegasus is also the symbol of those who strive to perfect their poetic gifts.

The Poqhirāj of Bengal is a flying horse similar to Pegasus.

THE PELICAN IN HER PIETY

The fabulous Pelican in her Piety is akin to the real aquatic bird but is endowed with mythical powers. The parent birds are devoted to their offspring, but the fledglings strike their parents in the face with their wings when they try to feed them. The Pelicans strike back in anger killing the young birds. Three days later the female Pelican pierces her breast and brings them back to life with her own blood. The Pelican's name means 'to pierce' – a word which originally applied to the woodpecker. It is not known why it was changed.

The Pelican in its Piety is one of the best known allegories of Christ. The Cathars embroidered the legend by giving it a foe, the night crow Nycticorox. The Pelican, who was described as the bird of light, left its fledglings in their nest in order to follow the sun. While she was away, Nycticorox wounded the young birds but fortunately the Pelican came back in time to cure them. It hid its light and remained in hiding near the nest and, sure enough, along came the night crow to complete its destruction of the baby birds. But in its turn it was struck down and killed by the Pelican. The Cathars used this tale to illustrate the Biblical story of how Christ had to lay aside his light to save mankind, surprised the devil at his evil work of corrupting humanity, and cast him into hell.

Some secret societies like the Rosicrucians have taken the Pelican opening her breast as their emblem, and in alchemy it represents one of the operations in the search for the Philosopher's Stone.

PELUDA

The Peluda, also known as the shaggy beast or La Velue, is said to have existed from before the flood. It had a serpent's head, the feet of a turtle and a round body covered in long green fur armed with poisonous quills. It terrorized the district around La Ferte-Bernard by emitting bursts of fire from its mouth that withered the crops. It also raided farmyards killing cattle and horses. When the farmers desperately hunted it, the Peluda flooded the surrounding area by plunging into the River Huisne. It died eventually when the lover of a maiden, who had become a victim of the monster, killed it by cutting its tail in two.

The coat of arms of the poet Johann Christoph Gottisched shows Pegasus, the creator of the fountain of poetical inspiration.

An illustration of the Beast.

Previous page
The Pelican in her Piety. From a fragment of 14th century AD glass.

The mortal foe of the human race – the Peryton.

PERYTON

In the sixteenth century a rabbi found a fragment of a treatise from the Alexandrian library that was destroyed by Oman. It contained a description of the savage Peryton who, it was believed, came from Atlantis. These creatures were half deer and half bird, combining the body, strong flying wings and plumage of a bird with the head and legs of a deer.

The shadow that the Peryton cast was very strange for its outline resembled that of a man and not its own. This aspect of the creature made the superstitious think that the Peryton was the spirit of a seafarer who had died away from home. The Peryton, as if denying this, was the mortal foe of the human race. If it succeeded in killing a man, its own shadow would return to it.

A story is told of how a wing of Perytons swooped down on those who came to conquer Carthage, killing and wounding many of them. No weapon was known that could kill a Peryton and the only thing that saved the remainder of the army was the fact that a Peryton can kill no more than a single man. The Erythraean Sibyl once foretold that the city of Rome would be destroyed by Perytons.

There were reported sightings of it over the Mediterranean islands and near the Straits of Gibraltar. The last time a Peryton was seen was in Ravenna. The report stated that its plumage was coloured pale blue which surprised many people, for the Peryton was supposed to have dark green feathers.

PHOENIX

See also Fêng Hwang, Senmurv.

The home of the Phoenix was Arabia where it lived alone in a sacred wood and fed only on pure air. It lived a solitary life for there is only one Phoenix alive, in the world, at any one time.

The word Phoenix in Greek means both 'a palm tree' or 'the colour purple' and most descriptions of this magnificent bird say that it is reddish purple in colour with a golden band around its neck. Other writers avow that its jewel-like plumage was coloured red, gold and blue and that its feathers had the power to heal any wound they touched. It was larger than an eagle and far more graceful and also had certain features of a pheasant. In alchemy, the Phoenix corresponds to the colour red, regeneration of universal life, and the successful completion of a process.

A Phoenix was supposed to live for over five hundred years although Pliny wrote that it survived for one thousand years. When the time came for it to die, it filled its wings with myrrh, laudanum, nard, cassia and cinnamon, and flew with them to Phoenicia. Here it selected the tallest palm tree that it could find and built a nest, out of the aromatic herbs, on top of the tree. It sat on its nest singing a song of rare beauty until the sun ignited the nest and burnt both bird and nest to ashes. But from the ashes there crept a small worm which grew into a new young Phoenix. When it was strong enough, the fledgling gathered up the remains of its

The Christian Phoenix from a floor mosaic at Daphne, Greece.

The Phoenix gathering aromatic herbs. From a medieval manuscript.

Two Bennu birds. From Egyptian papyri.

The head of a modern Piasa made of steel, and attached to the bluffs with strong beams.

parent, placed them inside a ball of myrrh and flew with the ball to Heliopolis in Egypt, the City of the Sun. A flight of birds followed it at a respectful distance. When the Phoenix had laid the ashes of the old Phoenix on an altar in the city, its duty to its parent was finished, and it flew back to its home until it was time for it too to die.

The Phoenix is the symbol of long life, agelessness, eternity, destruction and re-creation. It is the Christian sign of resurrection and eternal life; its capacity for rebirth was the reward for withstanding the temptation offered by Eve which made it also the symbol of steadfastness in the face of temptation.

The Turkish Phoenix is called Kerkes and in Egypt it is known as the Bennu.

The Bennu is the 'Bird of the Sun' who represents the sun dying in its own fire every night to rise again in the morning. Drawings of this bird show a grey or multi-coloured heron who utters the first sound at daybreak, calling the world back to life. It comes from the Isle of Fire in the Underworld bringing the vital Hike – the vital life force that is desired by all.

PIASA

Piasa in the American Indian Illini language means 'bird which devours men' but it should not be feared, for the only representations of a Piasa that are known are a modern, metal relief sculpture, and some sketches of an Algonquian Indian rock-painting first discovered on the Piasa rock near Alton, Illinois some centuries ago. There were originally two paintings of these strange creatures on the rock and these petroglyphs were described by the explorer Jacques Marquette in 1675:-

> "...as large as a calf; they had horns on their heads like those of a deer, a horrible look, red eyes, a beard like a tiger's, a face somewhat like a man's, a body covered with scales and so long a tail that it winds all round the body passing above the head and going back between the legs, ending in a fish's tail."

Part of the bluff which contained the petroglyphs must have eroded, for a drawing in 1854 shows only one creature and the head of another. This section of the rock was completely destroyed in 1846 or 1847. However, the community decided to preserve their Fabulous Beast, for in 1983, a Piasa was constructed of steel. It was decorated with bright, weather-resistant colours and fixed to the bluff with strong, steel beams.

The gentle, lunar Questing Beast.

THE QUESTING BEAST

The description of the Questing Beast occurs in 'Perlesvaus', translated into English from Old French as 'The High History of the Holy Grail'. Questing was originally the sound made by hounds when they found a scent.

"Josephus telleth us by the divine scripture that out of the forest issued a beast, white as driven snow, and it was bigger than a fox and less than a hare. The beast came into the launde all scared, for that she had twelve hounds in her belly that quested within like it were hounds in a wood, and she flew adown the launde for fear of the hounds the questing whereof she had within her. Percival rested on the shaft of his spear to look at the marvel of this beast, whereof he had right great pity, so gentle was she of semblance, and of so passing beauty, and her eyes it might seem that they were two emeralds. She runneth to the knight, all affrighted, and when she hath been there awhile and the hounds rend her again, she runneth to the damsel, but neither there may she stay long time, for the hounds that are within her cease not of their questing, whereof is she sore adread... The beast seeth that no protection hath she. She goeth to the cross, and forthwith might the hounds no longer be in her, but issued forth all as it were live hounds, but nought they had of her gentleness nor her beauty. She humbled herself much among them and crouched on the ground and made semblant as though she would have cried them mercy, and gat herself as nigh the cross as she might. The hounds had compassed her round about and ran in upon her upon all sides and tore her all to pieces with their teeth, but no power had they to devour her flesh, nor to remove it away from the cross."

106

This is a strange little tale, and is probably allegorical. Elizabeth Leader, in her work 'The Great Hound of the River Parrett', suggests that the beast who died to give place to twelve new hounds, could be a reference to a change in the calendar. The twelve hounds would represent the twelve months of the solar year which replaced the old lunar calendar. The colour of the Questing Beast certainly points to lunar associations as it is white.

A later description by Mallory gave it a serpent's head, the body of a Lybard, hare's feet, the buttocks of a lion and a noise in its belly like twenty couple of hounds questing. It appears in another guise in Edmund Spencer's 'Faerie Queene' as 'The Blatant Beast', the thousand-tongued symbol of malicious gossip.

RAINBOW MONSTER

The rainbow is one of the universal symbols of rain, an element which is particularly important in drought-ridden countries like Africa. So the first creature that Mawu, the Supreme Being of West African mythology, created was the Rainbow Serpent, the 'Divine Python' also known as Dan Ayido Hwedo. In the beginning everything was stagnant but Dan carried Mawu on his back all over the world. The tracks of his passing made the beds of rivers and the Serpent's excrement formed the mountain ranges. Mawu so enjoyed his trip that he became over-enthusiastic in his creativity and the earth was overburdened. Therefore he asked Dan to support the World by coiling himself into a circle with his tail in his mouth. Occasionally the Serpent moves, causing earthquakes. He can be glimpsed in the movement of a river and in the ripples of the sea that keeps him cool. He is seen in the lightning and the rainbow is his reflection. At night he is black, in the daytime white and is coloured red in the twilight. When the rainbow appears in the sky, it shows that the rainbow serpent is doing his duty by making sure that all the rivers and waterholes are sufficiently full to last throughout the next drought.

In the Congo, the Rainbow Monster is said to be a terrible animal that lives in the water and feeds on both humans and animals. Rainbows in the sky and in waterfalls are its reflection. On the Australian continent, rainbow serpents have names like Wulungu and Yülunggu. Their task in creation was also to carve out the rivers and watercourses of the country. In the Northwest territory of Australia, the Rainbow Serpent or Python is the consort of the Earth Mother. Aboriginal shamans will sit by the pool that is the home of

Rainbow Serpents. From an aboriginal painting.

a Rainbow Serpent and become possessed by the spirit of the reptile. When the shaman is under its hallucinatory influence, he can cure illnesses, know the future, and can call upon the clouds to let fall the life-giving rain.

RAVEN

Raven, who figures in the mythology of the Indians of the Northwest Pacific coastline of Canada, is an ambivalent figure. On one hand he is a culture hero, a great civiliser, the creator of the visible world, and on the other, he is a mischief-maker, lovable but irresponsible, sexy and delinquent.

Raven, the culture hero, is the bird who brought the Sun, Moon and Fire from Heaven to the people of the earth by his trickery and his ability to change his shape. In this guise he is shown in carvings with a red lump in his mouth to indicate fire. Raven, the supreme trickster, is equally admired by the Canadian Indians for his impudence and his ability to turn situations to his advantage, even in adversity. The following story of one of his adventures is a good example of this:

We-gyet – the Raven Trickster. A sketch of a print by Walter Harris. Kispiox, Canada. 1974.

Raven desired the comely wife of a fisherman and, in the guise of a handsome young redskin, persuaded her husband to look for some red feathers from a flock of birds who lived a short distance down the river. While the fisherman was away, Raven returned to the village and seduced the beautiful young wife, indulging in such erotic deeds that he was oblivious to the sound of the returning canoe. The husband chased Raven and beat him savagely. To save himself, Raven returned to his bird form with feathers of many different colours and a red crest on his head, but the man threw Raven's apparently lifeless body into the river where it was eaten by a halibut. The halibut, in its turn, was caught by a fisherman from another village who was astonished to see the marvellous bird inside the fish when he cut it open. However, Raven was still alive and changed himself into an old man who grew rapidly to the size of a giant. This so frightened the inhabitants of the village that they ran away leaving Raven to plunder their stores.

In Western countries the Raven is the harbinger of doom. In Ireland the Raven was the talisman of the war goddesses 'The Morrigan' and appeared before warriors who were fated to die in battle. It was credited with the powers of prophecy and the ability to see and know everything. The Raven was also the oracular bird of the Celtic hero Bran. The Norse god Odin owned two Ravens called Huginn and Muninn (Thought and Memory) who were his spies. They

Huginn and Muninn accompany a warrior.

Raven the Trickster. A
Bellacoola Indian mask.

flew around the world seeking out information for their
God. The Raven is the antithesis of the Pelican in her Piety.

In the 'Arabian Nights' the Raven Genius had a lion's face,
eagle's talons and eyes that showered forth sparks.

RE'EM

See also Unicorn.

There are references in the Hebrew Bible to the Re'em
which showed that it was a strange powerful creature believed to be the now extinct Auroch. Other sources write
that the Re'em was an ox as big as a mountain. Only two
existed, one male and one female, and as they lived far apart
in the East and the West, the Re'em only came together to
mate every seventy years. In the course of time the female
gave birth to twins, a male and a female, after which both
parents died.

REMORA

The fabulous Remora or Echeneis is a pale coloured fish
about thirty centimetres long which has a cartilaginous disk
on its head which acts as a sucker enabling it to attach itself

to any objects in its immediate surroundings. It is akin to the real sucking fish but has greater strength and tenacity, for the Remora has the power to attach itself to a ship and prevent it from moving. Pliny wrote that even the efforts of four hundred oarsmen could not make Caligula's ship move, once a Remora had attached itself to it. It is said to be traditionally associated with the cold, for it lived in polar regions. The chill of that place evaporated through the scales of the Remora made the area around the creature so cold, that any ship passing above it became so frozen that it could not move. Therefore the Remora is considered to be a preservative against scorching and is the enemy of the fire-loving Salamander. Remora, in Latin, means 'delay' or 'hindrance' and it was said that it could help a woman in pregnancy if it was applied outwardly to her womb, thus preventing a premature birth. Other writers describe the Remora as a docile amphibian easily tamed by sailors to help them catch other prey.

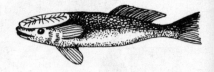

Drawing of a Remora, based on one in 'Les Monstres Marins' by A.Landrin. 1867.

ROC

Marco Polo's book of Travels and the 'Arabian Nights' both describe the Roc or Rukh Bird. Marco Polo believed that it lived in Madagascar off the east coast of Africa and had heard reports that it was shaped like an eagle. It was so immense that it could carry an elephant in its claws which it would kill by flying to a great height then dropping it to crash to its death on the rocks below. The wingspan of the Roc was forty paces long and its feathers were said to be as big as palm leaves. Some sources describe it as having two horns on its head and four humps; others say that it was half eagle and half lion making it a similar creature to the Griffin.

When Sinbad was stranded in a Roc's nest on top of a mountain, in the 'Arabian Nights', he found a Roc's egg as large as one hundred and forty- eight hen's eggs. When the adult returned, the adventurer was able to leave the confinement of the place by tying himself to the Roc's leg. He flew with it up into the sky so high that he lost sight of earth. But, eventually, he was able to escape when the Roc landed on another island where Sinbad found dry stream beds full of diamonds. Other synonyms of the Roc include the Chinese Pyong, the Russian Kreutzet and the Arabian Angka. According to Arabic tradition the Roc never lands on earth, only on the mountain Qaf, the centre of the world. However, reports of sightings of this bird cover the area from Greece to China. Symbolically it represents storms, wind and lightning.

The Bird and elephant

The Salamander living in the flames of a fire. From a 17th century alchemical text.

SALAMANDER

The Salamander is a creature that is well known in classical mythology and is also described in Bestiaries. It was a type of multi-coloured lizard that could live in the middle of a blazing fire and come to no harm, for it was able to extinguish flames. Pliny described it in his book of natural history as a reptile "so cold of complexion, that if he do but touch the fire, he will quench it as presently as if ice were put into it." This reptile was reputed to be extremely poisonous, its bite was said to be fatal, and if it touched and infected some fruit, any creature that ate the fruit would die.

Salamanders were often to be seen on the slopes of volcanos, especially when red hot lava was cascading down their slopes, but its natural habitat was the realm of Prester John. In the twelfth century, a letter, supposedly written by Prester John himself, was circulated which described the Salamander:-

"In one of our lands are worms called in our tongue Salamanders. These worms can only live in fire and they build cocoons like silk worms which are unwound by the ladies of our palace and spun into cloth and dresses, which are worn by our Exaltedness. These dresses in order to be cleaned and washed are cast into the flames."

This ability of cloth to remain intact when burnt seems to resemble the fireproof material asbestos. Asbestos can be made up into fireproof garments and has been known in past times as 'Salamander's Feather'.

The Salamander is a mythological fire spirit and the alchemical and graphic symbol of fire. As a heraldic creature, it is particularly famous because it

appears on the personal badge of Francis I of France. Here it is depicted as a lizard surrounded by flames with the inscription underneath 'I nourish the good and extinguish the bad'.

Pliny also described a small four-footed winged insect that was kin to the Salamander. This was the Pyrallis which lived in Cyprus in the copper furnaces and forges. If it emerged from the heat, it died.

SATYR

The earliest Satyr was a creature that was mainly human with a man's head, arms, body, legs and sexual organs. The rest of him was goat-like with a hairy skin, a tail, small horns on his head, pointed ears and a flattened nose. Originally he was the local spirit of a specific locality where he animated and personified the fruitfulness of the land.

In Egypt male goats were held in special reverence and Herodotus identified their divine he-goat as Pan, the Greek shepherd god of Hellenistic times. At this time the shape of the Satyr changed as it came under the influence of the type that is associated with Pan. The lower half of the Satyr from the waist downwards became completely goatlike and was the symbol not only of fecundity, but also of aggressive sexuality with its hairy animal lower part representing the vitality of base forces and instincts.

In Greece the Satyrs were depicted as the sons and attendants of the jovial and tipsy Silenus, the tutor of Dionysos. These attendants were usually drunk, cowardly, boastful womanizers and their names show some of the facets of their characters and appearance. For example: Simos (Snubnose), Posthon (Prick), Hybris (Insolence) and Komos (Revelry). However, they were relatively harmless and ridiculous, often behaving in an absurd and vulgar manner.

The Faun was the Roman equivalent of the Satyr and was the embodiment of the field and harvest spirits. He was generally portrayed as younger than the Satyr. Both the Satyr and the Faun represent lust, permissiveness and the powers of untamed nature.

SAWHORNED BEASTS

The Antalop is an animal that can be found in most medieval bestiaries. This fleetfooted creature had the body of a goat and long horns with a saw-like edge. It was even able to cut down trees with these horns. It was so exceedingly fierce that no hunter dared approach it and the only time that the Antalop could be captured was when it went

A faun-like fertility spirit. A wall decoration from the Sanctuary at Hatru, Assyria.

A Sawhorn Beast. An Antalop in a 12th century bestiary.

to drink at the River Euphrates. There it entangled its horns in the soft pliable branches of the Herecine plant that grew on the banks of the river. When the Antalop found that it was firmly caught by both horns, it called out in a loud voice which alerted the hunters to the fact that it was 'hors de combat'. It is interesting to note that the famous statues of 'The Goat in the Thicket' were found in the ruins of the ancient city of Ur, not so many miles from the River Euphrates.

The Calopus or Chatloup is a creature with spiky horns similar to the Antalop but, as its name suggests, it had a wolf-like body. It also managed to tangle its horns in thick undergrowth, and the Aeternae were Indian beasts who also had saw-edged bony horns on their foreheads. These they used in battle and were even able to defeat soldiers as the saw-like edges of the horn could cut through metal.

SCORPION MAN

In the Babylonian myth of creation, the monster Tiāmat gave birth to a host of grotesque creatures to help her in her battle against Marduk and the Gods. The Girtablulu or Scorpion Man was one of these creatures. He is described as of giant stature with a human head, arms, and legs, a scorpion's body and a stinging tail. The duty of Scorpion Man and his wife is to guard the gates at the entrance to the Mashu Mountain Range. When the hero Gilgamesh arrived at the mountains, Scorpion Man let him through, but issued the warning that no mortal had ever succeeded in crossing the range. In Mesopotamia and its adjacent regions, his likeness was carved on boundary stones and can be seen on Babylonian seals. In 'The Epic of Gilgamesh' the Scorpion Man represented Sagittarius and was considered to be only two thirds divine.

The Scorpion Man. From a Babylonian boundary stone.

SCYLLA

The story of Scylla and Charybdis can be found in Greek mythology and in 'The Odyssey' of Homer. Scylla was once a beautiful nymph, the daughter of Phorcys and Hecate Crataeis, although some say that Typhon and Echidne were her parents. She was changed into a fearful monster by Circe who was jealous of the God Glaucus's love for the nymph. Circe threw some magical herbs into the pool where Scylla bathed and, as soon as the nymph touched the water, she discovered to her horror that she had been transformed into a monster with twelve misshapen feet and six extremely long necks with a hideous head with a triple row of teeth on each of them. She concealed her body in a cave at the bottom

of a cliff with her six heads rearing up out of the chasm.

Charybdis was the daughter of Poseidon and Mother Earth. Zeus changed her into a whirlpool whose vortex was so strong that it could easily suck down a ship into the depths of the sea. She lived below a cliff that bore a green fig tree on its summit.

Homer tells the story about the perils that Odysseus had to face when he and his sailors steered their ship between the two cliffs, near the coast of Sicily, that were the homes of the monsters Scylla and Charybdis. Odysseus' ship had to draw close to the cliff where Scylla dwelt, in order to avoid the frightful whirlpool of Charybdis and, as he approached, her six heads shot out of the water, each whimpering hungrily like a new-born puppy. She swiftly snapped up a number of Odysseus's sailors and ate them with much cracking of bones. Odysseus escaped, but the two monsters remain ready to trap any more unwary sailors.

Scylla, based on a design from a coin from Agrigento, Sicily 420 – 415 BC.

SENMURV

Early depictions of the Senmurv show a creature that was a cross between a bird and a dog, and resembled a griffin. Her name is said to mean 'dog-bird' and she represents the elemental link between heaven and earth. Later depictions of the Senmurv make her much more like a bird with only the head, teeth and paws of a dog as well as the ability to suckle her young.

The Senmurv is a friend and benefactor of humanity for she is a fertility spirit. Her home is in the land where the Soma tree grows and where she is guarded by ninety nine thousand, nine hundred and ninety nine attendants and a

A Sassanid-Persian Senmurv.

113

114

Cernunnos, whose
Ram-headed serpent
companion is duplicated.
Stonecarving from
Cirencester, England.

A late Bronze Age
Hathor/Astarte plaque
from Canaan.

supernatural fish. The tree where the Senmurv roosts is immortal and carries the seeds of all the wild plants of the earth. When the Senmurv alights on her tree, the weight of her body shakes the tree's branches, scattering down all the seeds that were ripening there. The Chamrosh, a similar creature often confused with the Senmurv, gathers up the seeds and spreads them over the ground.

In later Persian folklore, the Senmurv was known as the Simurg and was described as a giant bird that nested on the highest peak of the Alburz mountains in northern Persia. A Simurg's feather could be used for healing purposes. The Simargl, Simyr and Sinam are related to the Senmurv and all are beneficient to mankind.

SERPENT

See also Dragon, Vouivre, Worm

Ophiolatary – the worship of the serpent – can be traced back many centuries into prehistory. Both the shape and the habits of the serpent make it a meaningful symbol of fertility. The sloughing of its skin, giving it periodic rebirth, denotes not only reincarnation but also the cyclic changes of the moon and the hidden re-energising powers of the earth in spring. Although the serpent is a creature of natural history and not a creature of fantasy, the magical powers attributed to it when it was worshipped, allows it to be considered as fabulous. Serpents are the guardians of the springs of life and immortality and also of the superior riches of the spirit symbolized by hidden treasure.

Sacred Serpents figure in many creation myths. In India, the serpent was associated with the God Vishnu. Ananta 'the Infinite', also known as 'the Serpent of Infinity' and as Sesha, acted as a couch for the Hindu God when he slept during the intervals of creation. Sesha represented the primary life force of cosmic water and was portrayed with many heads like a Hydra.

In the Pelasgian myth of creation, the Universal Goddess Eurynome created the great serpent Ophion to become her mate. Soon Eurynome became pregnant and gave birth to the 'Universal Egg'. Ophion coiled around the egg until it hatched, and out fell everything that exists in the universe from the sun to the smallest ant. Eurynome and Ophion made their home on Mount Olympus, but Ophion grew vainglorious and boasted that he was the author of the whole of creation. This enraged Eurynome who hit him over the head with the heel of her shoe, kicked out his teeth and threw him into the dark caves beneath the earth.

The people of Egypt worshipped their supreme goddess in the form of a cobra calling her Ua Zit (Great Serpent), and the Goddess Hathor was identified with the poison-spitting man- killing Uraeus serpent when she violently destroyed rebellious mankind in her efforts to protect Re, the ageing god of the sun. The serpent of Hathor was such a powerful symbol that the Pharaoh of Egypt appropriated it for himself and placed it on his crown to show that he, as Re's living representative, was under the care of the Goddess.

The Uraeus was not only the sign of the Goddesses' protection, it was also identified with the falcon warrior Horus. Again Re was threatened by his enemies and this time took protective action by sending Horus, in the form of a winged disc, to slay his foes. When Horus assumed the form of the winged disc, i.e. the sun of Re equipped with his own falcon wings, he added to it two fire-spitting Uraeus serpents. The winged disc was then the God himself and a weapon of destruction as it flew from the heavens like a bolt of destroying fire to eliminate the enemies of Re. The winged disc, composed of sun, wings and serpents, can be found in the Middle East, Egypt, Mexico, Hindustan, Greece, Italy and occasionally China. It is the triple symbol of serpent, sun and wings representing the Deity as Creator, Preserver and Destroyer.

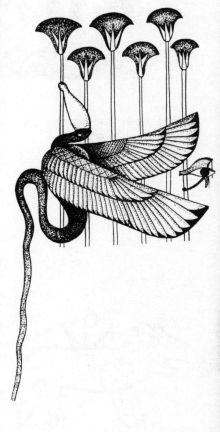

The Uraeus Serpent. From an Egyptian papyrus.

From the Egyptian 'Book of the Coming Forth into Day' comes the description of the serpent Ka-en-Ankh Nereru, known as 'The Life of the Gods'. In the twelfth hour of the night the God Re, in his boat, is shown being pulled completely through Ka-en-Ankh Nereru; the boat enters at the serpent's tail in total darkness bearing the God in the form of the extinguished old Sun. When the boat emerges through the serpent's mouth into day, the god comes forth young and alive. The progress of the Sun God through the serpent symbolizes at one level the purifying of the soul through wisdom. The serpent, like the dragon who evolved from it, represents wisdom or enlightenment.

Python, the serpent who gave oracles in the name of Ge or Themis (the Earth Goddess) once a year at the Shrine of Delphi, was so huge that the coils of its body covered a great stretch of the countryside. The serpent was killed by the archer-god Apollo who almost emptied his quiver in his efforts to destroy the creature. The Pythian Games which Apollo instigated are the funeral rites of Python and it is said that its bones and teeth were kept in the kettle upon the sacred tripod in the shrine and its hide was wrapped around the tripod itself.

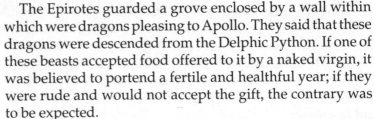

'The souls of the damned in torment.' A mosaic in the Baptistry in Florence, Italy.

A benign Agathos Daimon.

The Epirotes guarded a grove enclosed by a wall within which were dragons pleasing to Apollo. They said that these dragons were descended from the Delphic Python. If one of these beasts accepted food offered to it by a naked virgin, it was believed to portend a fertile and healthful year; if they were rude and would not accept the gift, the contrary was to be expected.

Propitiating serpents or dragons with food was not confined to sacred groves. Because of their habit of disappearing and appearing from cracks in the earth, serpents were believed to be the souls of the departed come back to visit the living. Therefore small non-poisonous snakes called Dracunculi – little dragons – were made welcome within the home, offered bread and milk and addressed as 'Master of the House', thus ensuring good fortune to the residence.

The Agathos Daimon is the Phoenician version of the Sacred Serpent; sometimes it is called the Agatha Demon. This little creature can be identified by its heart-shaped tongue and wings. It is similar to the benevolent 'Genius Serpents' that can be seen painted on the walls of household shrines in Pompeii and other Roman cities. The Agathos Daimon was believed to be an invisible winged serpent hovering around mankind.

The Ouroboros is a serpent or dragon biting its own tail and is the symbol of self-fecundation, nature returning within a cyclic pattern to its own beginning. Sometimes it is drawn with its body half light and half dark, symbolizing the counterbalancing of opposing principles similar to the Chinese Yin – Yang symbol. In alchemy, one Venetian manuscript depicted the Ouroboros with its body half black representing earth and night and the other half white indicating heaven and light.

The magical powers attributed to the Serpent are not always beneficial. The ambivalence of its symbolism can be seen in the way it can be regarded as a source of wisdom and fertility and can at the same time represent evil and destruction. The Guivre, a serpent with the head of a dragon, and the Amphiptere, a winged serpent, were both the enemies of humanity as was the Italian Boa who clung to the udders of buffalo and oxen, destroying the cattle by sucking them dry.

The serpent has evil attributes in various religions. In India, the Weather God Indra vanquished the serpent demon Vitra who encompassed the waters of chaos and kept them from fertilising the earth; he released the earth's lifegiving water and cast Vitra into outer darkness. The Cosmic Serpent in Egyptian myths is a potent enemy when it appears as the serpent- devil Apopis who represents the powers of darkness, before its defeat by the Sun God Re. In the Christian religion the snake is referred to as, "that old serpent, the devil" and is cast into the underworld. When it is chthonic, the serpent often represents dark negative force and is the enemy of the light and the sun.

A mythical creature usually described as a 'lion' in combat with a serpent, from the Jelling Rune Stone, Denmark.

SIREN

See also Harpy, Mermaid

In Greek mythology, the Sirens were the daughters of the muse Terpsichore and either Achelous, the River God, or Phorcys, the Sea God. Some say that there were two Sirens, others that there were three or four. Their names described their musical abilities, for one was called Thelxiepeia – her of the charming voice, and another one had the name of Aglaophones – her of the splendid voice.

They were the companions of the young goddess Core, afterwards called Persephone when she was abducted by Hades, the king of the underworld. Demeter, Core's mother, changed these beautiful maidens into golden-plumaged birds to punish them for not looking after her child. It is also claimed that the maidens themselves asked for this metamorphosis so that they could fly across the seas in order to search for the young Goddess. The Gods would not permit the seductive melodies that fell so sweetly from the lips of the Sirens to be silenced and permitted them to retain their human heads and voices. Aphrodite is also reputed to have changed these musicians into birds to punish them for their pride, for they would not sacrifice their maidenhood to any

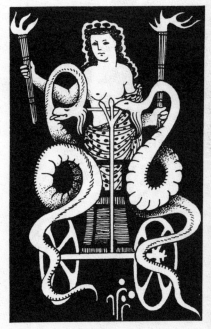

Medea in her serpent chariot. 5th century AD.

This figure was described as a Siren in the Roxburgh Bestiary.

A Siren. From a fragment of Greek pottery.

god or man.

Later the Sirens were even deprived of the powers of flight, for the Muses defeated them in a musical contest. They pulled out the Sirens' wing feathers to make crowns for themselves, thus forcing them to live on an island called Anthemoessa where they sat and sang in a green meadow surrounded by heaps of sailor's bones. These sailors had been lured to their deaths by the song of the Sirens which no man could resist. Lycophron called these creatures 'barren nightingales' and 'slayers of centaurs' because their music was so intoxicating that the centaurs even forgot to eat.

One day Jason and his Argonauts were passing the island, in their ship, when they heard the song of the Sirens. But they paid no attention to it, for the sound of Orpheus's lute drowned their song with his far sweeter music. It has been told that the Sirens committed suicide when they failed to lure Jason to them, but they were still on their island when Odysseus passed by a generation later. Odysseus, warned by the witch Circe, had himself tied to the mast of his ship and his sailors plugged their ears with wax. Although he struggled like a madman to reach the Sirens, his bonds held and this time the Sirens did commit suicide for nothing has been heard of them since.

The Sirens are the personification of temptation and feminine seduction, capable of distracting men from their goals in life and leading them to their spiritual death. They represent the illusions that are obtained through the seductive powers of the senses and their attributes are lyres and flutes. Although Sirens are generally portrayed as human-headed birds, sometimes they are depicted with a fishtail. Distinctions between Mermaids and Sirens are often very blurred.

In mythology, Anthemoessa, the land of the Sirens, is regarded as the sepulchral island which receives the dead, and the Sirens are the servants of the death goddess. For this reason pairs of Sirens can be found carved on tombs, carrying the souls of the deceased. Sirens, like their cousins the Harpies, were considered to be birds of prey who waited to catch and secure the souls of the dead.

SLEIPNIR

See also Hippocamp

Sleipnir, the eight-legged stallion, was the steed of the Norse God Odin (Germanic Tiwas, Anglo-Saxon Woden) the wild horseman who rode across the sky at the head of his host of dead warriors. Some farmers left their last sheaf of grain for Sleipnir hoping that the hunt would pass by without injuring them, for it was the hunt of death and people could be swept up in it and carried away. In France its leader was the Grand Huntsman of Fontainebleau and in England he was Herne the Hunter.

Some authorities on old Norse legends think that both Odin and his steed were originally identical, together personifying the powers of darkness and death. A carving on a gravestone from Tjangride in Gothland represents a man riding on an eight-legged horse and either represents Odin riding his horse Sleipnir, or figures a dead man being carried away by the Horse God.

Odin is often attributed with the qualities of a shaman, a priest or psychopomp who cures sickness, directs sacrifice and escorts the souls of the dead to the other world. The shaman has a close affinity with horses because he, himself, will sacrifice a horse offered to the Gods and in spirit escort the animal's soul aloft. He obtains admission to the higher planes in this way, to seek aid for the community which he serves. Sleipnir, as Odin's steed, draws attention to the shaman's powers of sending his soul in swift flight to heaven.

Sleipnir not only carries the dead to heaven, he is also capable of travelling to the underworld where Hel reigns. When Baldeur the Beautiful, the favourite of the Gods, was murdered by a mistletoe shaft, Hermod the son of Odin rode Sleipnir to Hel in the underworld and offered her a ransom for the return of the God.

SPHINX

The Egyptian Androsphinx, given this name to distinguish it from the Greek Sphinx, is one of the oldest of the fabulous beasts. It has a human head and the body of a lion lying at rest. This juxtaposition of a human head and an animal's body shows that the Sphinx is not to be considered as a real animal but as a being endowed with special powers characteristic of both humans and animals; the human head is the intelligence that controls the force of the lion's body. The Androsphinx, with its head carved into the likeness of a Pharaoh, represents the physical and spiritual powers that are incarnate in not only the Pharaoh, but also in his government, the royal priesthood.

There are statues of many different types of Sphinx to be seen in Egypt. The most important are the Criosphinx who has a lion's body and the head of a ram, it represents silence and was worshipped as a symbol of Amun whose soul was

The eight-legged stallion Sleipnir on a gravestone from Tjangride, Gothland.

A heraldic emblem showing a modern example of an Andro-sphinx.

The Greek Sphinx quizzes Oedipus. A design from a piece of pottery.

believed to be enshrouded in it, and the Hieracosphinx who has the head of a falcon and represents the solar power of the God Horus. According to the astromythology of the Egyptians, the Androsphinx at Giza was called Hor-em-akhen which means Horus of the Horizon, in Greek 'Harmachis'.

Not all of the Egyptian Sphinx are masculine. A slightly older Androsphinx than the one at Giza has female features, possibly representing the Goddess Hathor. But there can be no doubt about the femininity of the Greek Sphinx as the head is clearly female and her lion's body generally carries human breasts. She is described as having the head of a woman, the body of a lion, the tail of a serpent and the wings of an eagle. She is the symbol of destruction, the enemy of mankind and also the supreme embodiment of the enigma, guarding the ultimate meaning that is forever beyond man's understanding.

The Sphinx, who was reputed to be the daughter of the serpent monster Echidne and either Typhon or Orthrus, was sent by the Gods to the Greek city of Thebes in Bocotia to punish it for the crimes of its king. She sat on a clifftop outside the city and waylaid travellers who passed by with demands for an answer to her riddle. "What creature with only one voice walks on four legs in the morning, two at noon and three in the evening?" Those who were unable to answer her riddle were promptly throttled. The Greek word for Sphinx means strangler.

Oedipus fled to Thebes in an effort to escape from the prophesy that he would kill his father and marry his mother. Not unexpectedly, he was accosted by the Sphinx who demanded an answer to her riddle. "Man," he replied. "He crawls when he is a baby, stands upright in his prime and leans on his staff when he is old." The Sphinx, mortified by his correct answer, threw herself to her death on the rocks below.

The Greeks used a portrait of the Sphinx on military ensigns and flags in memory of the oedipean monster, and effigies of her were used for funerary purposes. It is thought that the image of the Greek Sphinx was derived from a representation of the winged Moon Goddess of Thebes or figures of the human-headed lion which may have infiltrated from Egypt. Astrologers consider that the Sphinx is an astrological symbol and a calendar beast. The female head corresponds to Virgo the virgin, and the body to Leo the lion. The Sphinx that is depicted with a human face, a bull's body, a lion's legs and the wings of an eagle, represents the fixed signs of the zodiac Aquarius, Taurus, Leo and Scorpio.

The warrior Tengū – half bird, half human.

TENGŪ

The Tengū are goblin birds, half bird and half human; they have claws like those of a giant eagle, glowing eyes and a long red beak. Their bird characteristics are those of a kite; the Garunda and the T'ien Kou were said to be its ancestors.

These creatures are the persecutors of Buddhists. Priests who practised hypocrisy have to accept the punishment of walking the 'Tengū Road'. This means that each turns into a Tengū who has to swallow a ball of red hot metal three times a day as a punishment for misdemeanours. Fortunately for them, the pain soon subsides and the Tengū can then plan how to cause war and ferment unrest, for the main objective of a Tengū is to cause trouble. Their home was a fortress north of Kyoto on Mount Kurama and it was here that the Tengū tried to bedevil the world by teaching man to use the weapons of war. Japanes Samurai revered the Tengū for their mastery of the martial arts and of the warrior's spirit. A mortal who came in close contact with one of these supernatural creatures was blessed with the ability to absorb some of their power. The Tengū are the symbols of war and conflict.

Nowadays they are regarded as bird-like spirits who steal children and play pranks on the unsuspecting.

THUNDERBIRD

The Thunderbird plays a prominent part in many North American mythologies. It is a universal spirit associated with dynamic sky powers, especially those connected with the weather. It is generally portrayed as a gigantic bird similar to an eagle, who lives in the upper regions of clouds and winds,

The Red Indian
Thunderbird and Halibut.
A woodcarving from
Southern Kwakiutl, British
Columbia, Canada.

signalling its presence by flashing the lightning of its eyes
or by the thunder of its beating wings and shaking tail.

Harney Peak, the highest mountain in the Black Hills of
Dakota, was, according to the Sioux Indians, the home of
the Thunderbird Waukheon. This peak would receive the
brunt of the bird's anger if the Sioux people ever strayed
from the ways of their ancestors. However, the Sioux considered that the Thunderbird was a wise creature who did
no harm, although its fledglings could be irresponsible and
cause damage. At Eneti, in Washington State, a face said to
be that of a Thunderbird is carved on a rock; if the rock is
shaken, the Thunderbird will become enraged and rain will
fall. The Pawnee Indians use a medicine bundle called a
'storm eagle' – a dead eagle stuffed with magical objects – in
order to raise storms.

The shape of the Thunderbird differs slightly among the
North American tribes. The Dakota Indians say that they
killed a Thunderbird and discovered that it had the face of
a man and an eagle's beak. The Northwest Coast Indians
describe the Thunderbird as vast enough to carry a whole
lake on its back and strong enough to carry off and eat a
whole whale leaving only its bones on the mountain tops.

The Nimpkish Indians have a creation myth regarding
the Thunderbird who, as well as being a supernatural bird,
had the ability to change itself into human shape. It lived on
a high mountain as a human and put on its bird form in
order to hunt whales.

After the great flood, the Halibut swam ashore at the
mouth of the Nimpkish River, assumed human form and
began to build a house. As he struggled to raise the massive
house beams, Halibut realized that he had not the necessary
strength to complete his task. In despair, he called aloud for
assistance and was heard by the Thunderbird who flew

down from his mountain to aid the fish-man. He picked up the great beams easily with his giant claws and put them in place. When the house was finished, Thunderbird assumed human form and vowed that he would be Halibut's younger brother. These two were the first of the Nimpkish people.

TIĀMAT

See also Dragon

The imperfect fusion of the traditions of Babylonian and Egyptian mythology form the basis of one of the most complete legends of a hero's fight with a dragon. The story of the Babylonian genius was discovered on seven tablets which were brought to light by the British excavations on the site of Nineveh. They date from the second millennium BC and were originally composed in Akkadian, the umbrella name for the various Babylonian and Assyrian dialects. When they were translated, the story of the dragoness Tiāmat and her slayer Marduk was unfolded. Tiāmat is portrayed as a dragoness with a serpent-like body, horns, forelegs, a long tail, and a hide that weapons could not pierce.

Enuma Elish – the Babylonian genesis – began with a chaos of water which contained two living beings, male and female, Apsu and Tiāmat, who mated and brought forth Anshar and Kishar (Heaven and Earth) who in their turn also produced offspring. As the numbers of the Gods increased, they began to annoy Apsu who plotted to destroy them. The Gods found out and killed Apsu, leaving Tiāmat to live on in her own element, brooding over the death of her husband. Eventually she formed an alliance with Kingu to make war against the reigning Gods. She produced reinforcements for the battle to come, giving birth to eleven kinds of fearsome beasts including Scorpion Men and creatures called Lahamu. The god Marduk was the only one who was not afraid and agreed to fight Tiāmat. Armed with a bow and arrows, a mace, lightning and a net of the four winds, Marduk advanced to meet his monstrous enemy. From the Epic of Creation comes this description of the battle:-

Tiamat.

> They marched to war, they drew near to give battle.
> The Lord spread out his net and caught her in it.
> The evil wind which followed him, he loosed it in her face.
> She opened her mouth, Tiāmat, to swallow him.
> He drove in the evil wind so that she could not close her lips.
> The terrible winds filled her belly, her heart was seized.

She held her mouth wide open.
He let fly an arrow, it pierced her belly.
Her inner parts he clove, he split her heart.
He rendered her powerless and destroyed her life.
He felled her body and stood upright upon it.

Then out of Tiāmat's body Marduk created earth and sky, the world order that we know, then Kingu's veins were opened and from his blood mankind was created. Symbolically Tiāmat represents primeval chaos, water and darkness.

George Michanowsky in his book 'The Once and Future Star', writes of the incongruity of the statement that the primordial sea, which in Sumerian belief brought forth the world around us without conflict, has here been recast in the image of a violent demon who had to be destroyed. The unhinging transformation of a benign symbol of lifegiving cosmic water into an all-devouring monster; the Babylonian superimposition of a deep-seated male – female conflict onto a serene creation tradition, provided a discordant distortion for which western culture would have to pay a very high price. He considers that the story may partially be explained as a history of a very real encounter when the Babylonians conquered the Sea Country of Lower Mesopotamia, an area called Mat Tamtim. This required the official creation story to be rewritten to meet the propaganda requirements of the new order and then projected back into mythical time.

A head believed to be that of Tiamat. From a Babylonian boundary stone.

TOAD

See also Basilisk, Cockatrice

J. E. Cirlot considers that the Toad is the inverse and infernal aspect of the frog symbol and writes that in esoteric thought :-

"There are also certain animals whose mission it is to break up the astral light by a process of absorption peculiar to them. There is something fascinating about their gaze; they are the Toad and the Basilisk."

The three-legged toad is the companion of the Chinese Immortal Liu-hai who caught the magical beast one day when drawing water from a well. This toad is one of the symbols of Yin (passivity, femininity and the dark part of the Yin Yang symbol) which makes its master extremely powerful. Liu-hai often carries a string of coins as he is the patron of commercial success. In Chile, the Strong Toad has a turtle shell on its back which glows in the dark. There is something bewitching about its gaze that can attract or repel.

A God on the Toad.

A woodcarving of a resting Unicorn.

UNICORN
See also Bull, Re'em, Ch'i-lin

The Unicorn is one of the most ancient of mythological beasts for its history can be traced back to the earliest written traditions of ancient Mesopotamia, where its original shape was that of a bull with a forward crumpled horn. This bull was akin to the Unicorn that occupied a prominent position on the early Indian seals of the Harappa period. In Babylon, pictures of the Unicorn showed an animal with a slim body which resembled that of a horse and that, in turn, was followed in Assyrian art by a Unicorn with a goat- like body. The Unicorn has also been represented in East Asia and Islamic art, but there has been no continuity of visual representation down through classical antiquity. It is only in the literature of the Greek and Roman eras that allusions to the Unicorn are found. The Greek historian Ctesias described the Unicorn, which he called Onyx Monoceros, as a very swift wild ass with a white coat, a purple head, blue eyes and a horn in the middle of its forehead. This horn had a white base, a red tip and the middle was black. It is likely that this exotic creature was derived from Tibetan and Himalayan traveller's tales about the Ch'i-lin, the Unicorn of China.

Pliny, a later historian than Ctesias, described a totally different creature which had the body of a horse, the head of a stag, the feet of an elephant and the tail of a boar. It had a single black horn three feet long projecting from its forehead and it uttered a deep bellow. This account was so clear that it is widely thought that Pliny was describing a rhinoceros and that all descriptions of the Unicorn stemmed from this factual beast. However, this explanation is too simplistic, for Pliny's description, although possibly taken from

The Unicorn. From a
'millefleur' tapestry of 'La
Dame a la Licorne', Musee
de Cluny, France.

older sources, is preceded by a number of others quite
different in content. Also illustrations from the Near East
and the previously mentioned Harappa seals show the ge-
nuine rhinoceros and the Unicorn, as a different beast,
standing together. Therefore it would appear that it is justi-
fied to call a one-horned creature by the name Unicorn,
unless of course, a rhinoceros is clearly and faithfully depicted.

It is likely that the Unicorn found its way into European
mythology via the crusaders returning from the Holy Wars
in Syria and Palestine. It became a popular addition to the

Bestiaries of the Middle Ages. In the Bestiaries, the Unicorn differed very little from the description given of it by Ctesias. The head and body were more like those of a horse than an ass, its forelegs were those of an antelope and its overall colour was white. Topsell says of it:-

"They keep for the most parts in the deserts and live
solitary in the tops of mountains. There was nothing
more horrible than the braying of it, for the voice was
strained above measure. It fighteth both with the
heeles, with the mouth biting like a lyon, and with
the heeles kicking like a horse."

The Unicorn is a fleet and wary creature and can be fierce if cornered. In Isidore of Seville's Etymologies of the seventh century AD, he reported that one thrust of a Unicorn's horn can kill an elephant. It will attack its predators with its sharp and lethal horn, but if its horn should get stuck in a tree trunk, thus trapping it, then it can be easily slaughtered.

It is such a difficult creature to catch that, according to the myths of the Middle Ages, the only way to snare it was to persuade a virgin maiden to sit down near the Unicorn's hunting ground. The Unicorn approached and leapt into her lap. She fondled it and warmed it with her love and soon it was willing to accompany her wherever she wished to go even if death awaited it. This myth clearly shows a phallic motif and, because the Unicorn's association with the virgin maiden indicated that their relationship was of a lascivious nature, powdered Unicorn horn was considered to be a powerful aphrodisiac. The Unicorn also provided a useful metaphor to the erotic verse of the period. A poem by Thibaut, Count of Champagne, in 'Poesies du roi de Navarre' likens its author to a Unicorn:-

The Unicorn and I are one:
He also pauses in amaze
Before some maiden's magic gaze,
And, while he wonders, is undone.
On some dear breast he slumbers deep,
And Treason slays him in that sleep.
Just so have ended my life's days;
So Love and my Lady lay me low.
My heart will not survive the blow.

In mythology, man has often persecuted the Unicorn mainly for the magical and medicinal qualities of its horn. It is said that the horn, when dipped in water, repels venomous creatures and it is for this reason that other animals around a water hole will let the Unicorn drink first because, when the horn touches the water, it becomes pure. If powdered Unicorn horn is drunk, the recipient will not suffer

A Unicorn – part of a playing card by the Master E.S.

from spasms, epilepsy or be poisoned. The horn represents
the power of the beast and physicians used to supply rhinoceros horn, representing it to be the horn of a Unicorn, to
be used as a medicament. Oryx or Narwhal horns were also
used to counterfeit the horn of the Unicorn. The Narwhal is
called the 'Sea Unicorn' because its hard, white, convoluted
horn resembles those seen in illustrations of Unicorns.

The Unicorn is one of the most popular of the heraldic
beasts and is seen in the Royal Arms of England where it
appears with the lion. These two animals are often illustrated in combat with each other. Each strives to dominate
the other and the outcome was believed to follow a seasonal
pattern. In spring the Unicorn's power was at its greatest,
but in summer, the lion won suzerainty. Symbolically the
fight between a real beast and a fabulous one represented
the conflict between realistic and fanciful tendencies.

Other names that are used for the Unicorn include Licorn,
Alicorn, Biasd Na Srognig and Abath. The Karkadan should
be included in this list, as its history is very similar to that
of the Unicorn. The Karkadan was a Persian or Indian
monster that had the shape of a gigantic rhinoceros and was
capable of carrying off an elephant on its great horn. This
solitary and ferocious predator was the enemy of humanity.
It was far more aggressive than the Unicorn, but it could
also be tamed by a young virgin and the sweet voice of the
ring dove had a calming effect upon it. A knife handle made
of Karkadan horn would tremble violently in the presence
of poison; the enemies of the Borgias would have found this
tool very useful.

VOUIVRE

See also Melusine, Sacred Serpent, Wyvern

The Vouivre is a French Wyvern which is usually portrayed with the head and upper body of a voluptuous
woman. She has a ruby or a garnet set into her head between
the eyes, or possibly in place of them, with which she is able
to guide herself through the underworld. In some traditions
this precious eye is a luminous ball that hangs in the air in
front of the reptile. The only chance to rob the Vouivre of
her jewel is when she is bathing and leaves the stone un-
guarded, resting on the ground. If that should happen, she
would be as blind as a glass worm.

Jousserandot called the Vouivre the good 'Genius', the
friend of liberty who hovers protectively over the highlands
and the countryside. She lived in mountainous regions, in
ruins and in abandoned chateaux and also frequented the

A spotted Wyvern.

Nivernais, the area around Nevers, where her name was transformed into 'Wivre'. Here she guarded many treasures. The Vouivre was also known in Switzerland and Germany where she retained her familiar aspects and role: that of a winged aquatic creature who carried a jewel and was female. It was said in some quarters that 'Melusine' was a Vouivre and that both reptile and woman/serpent were in rapport with the telluric currents of the earth. Louis Charpentier had this to say about the Vouivre in 'The Mysteries of Chartres Cathedral':-

> "To men of the 20th century such a phrase as 'the spirit that breathes or inspires' may sound childish; but this is only because metaphors and images have changed. One can designate 'Spirit' in learned enough terms, but it would be a pity not to recall the old Gaulish name for it, Wouivre.

> "The Wouivre has been personified in different ways, which are simply poetic images. It is the name our ancestors gave at the same time to snakes that glide on the ground and, by extension, to rivers that 'snake', such as the Wouivre, and to currents that 'snake' through the ground. Today we call these 'telluric'. Some of them spring from the movement of subterranean waters; others from faults which have brought soils of different kinds into contact, which develop differences of potential according to changes of temperature; some, again, flow from the depths of terrestrial magma.

> "These currents are a manifestation of a life that goes on deep in the Earth herself and where they fail to reach, the soil is dead, without fecundity, as a part of the human body would be if it were no longer irrigated by the blood-stream. Contrary-wise, they carry to those places where they are found a fresh supply of life which makes the earth fruitful. These are places which the 'snakes' seek as it were of their own will, whence perhaps this likening of the currents with the serpents they symbolise.

> "What is more, and doubtless by way of analogy, the ancients gave the name 'Wouivres' to the currents that today we term cosmic, or at least magnetic. They represented them by winged serpents and sometimes birds: the 'Sirens' often shewn as birds with women's faces. Places where telluric and aerial currents met and by their very nature, gave birth to flying dragons and such: the 'Melusines', or women that are half snake."

Vouivre, the French Wyvern.

A female Werewolf wrapped in a mantle of soft, white fur.

WEREWOLF

The legends of the Werewolf, also known as the Vircolac, Loup Garou or Vulkodlac can be found in Europe, the Balkans and Russia. They relate the stories of one of the most ancient of man's superstitions, the metamorphosis of man into wolf. Werewolves were feared in Ancient Greece where lycanthropy – the gradual changing of man into beast – was referred to as 'lupinam insanium' which literally means wolf madness. In fact the word lycanthropy itself is derived from the Greek 'luk anthropia', meaning wolf man.

The condition of lycanthropy was one that could strike anyone, anywhere, in any walk of life, at any time, although it occurred most often at the time of the full moon. A bite inflicted by a lycanthrope could also turn its victim into another Werewolf. A true Werewolf not only looks like a wolf but also considers him or herself to be one. When the change from man to beast occurs, the human features blur and coarsen, the body and palms of the hands become covered with fur, the eyes redden and glow, the nose runs, the mouth salivates, speech is replaced by guttural sounds and the Werewolf drops to an animal position on all fours with its nails extended into claws. Werewolves can be both male and female. Some of the most lethal are female and legends about female Werewolves tend to assume sexual overtones.

In the story of 'The White Wolf of Kostepchin' by Sir Gilbert Cambell, a 19th century novelist, he describes a female Werewolf:-

> *"As the bushes divided, a fair woman wrapped in a*
> *mantle of soft white fur with a fantastically shaped*
> *travelling cap of green velvet upon her head, stood*

Head of a Werewolf. From an engraving by the French artist Jacques Callot of Nancy.

before them. She was exquisitely fair and her long titian red hair hung in dishevelled masses over her shoulders."

This alluring creature is immediately given refuge by a dissolute nobleman who asks for her hand in marriage. The girl demands his heart and when he agrees, leaps upon him tearing that organ from his breast and devouring it.

The lycanthrope is both the villain of its metamorphosis and its victim for when it returns to human shape, the remembrance of the foul murders it has performed while in the form of a wolf will continually haunt it. It is small wonder that, by day, it is stricken with remorse, for the usual way for a Werewolf to kill is by biting through the jugular vein of its victim and feasting on the remains. The only hope and cure for a Werewolf is death and this could be very unpleasant unless it is lucky enough to be shot and killed instantly. The Werewolf could only be destroyed in certain ways. In early times it could be dispatched by fire or a sword, but later the most usual way to kill the beast was to shoot it, using a silver bullet preferably made from a silver crucifix.

The legends about Werewolves were totally believed by the people who lived in mountainous and rural districts of France, Germany and Eastern Europe, where wolves were a common menace. A dreadful end befell anyone who the local populace suspected of being a Werewolf. The accused was either burnt alive or beheaded. Sometimes, in order to see if the accusation was true, the suspect Werewolf was cut open to see if the wolf's fur was on the inside of its skin, as many people believed that a Werewolf could reverse its skin in order to avoid recognition.

J. E. Cirlot writes that the Werewolf is the symbol of the irrationality latent in the baser parts of humanity and the possibility of its awakening. This is also true of the Werepanther, Weretiger and Werejaguar who present similar types of metamorphosis, the human changing into the named animal. The Weretiger is particularly common in the legends of the Orient.

WORM

See also Dragon, Midgard's Worm, Serpent, and Hippocamp

Worm is the name given to dragons of Northern Europe who have a serpentine shape without wings or legs. The words Worm, Orm or Vurm come from the Norse word 'ormr' which means dragon. These creatures are kin to the sacred and demonic serpents who also had simple snake-like forms.

In mythology, the Worm, unlike the dragon, had no redeeming features. It was described as a great goggle-eyed slimy serpent with foul breath, and was even uglier than a leech. It was portrayed in carvings and manuscripts, especially in early pictures of St. George or St. Michael killing the dragon, with a horned, reptilian or horse-like head on the end of a completely serpentine body. This gigantic serpent was reputed to move with great speed, propelling

The Gurt Vurm of Shervage Wood.

134

Left: An Ethiopian St. George who is also slaying a great Worm.

Right: St. George slaying a worm-like Dragon. From a 12th century tympanum at Brinsop Church. England.

itself along with coiling thrusts of its great body. Its natural habitat was in wet or damp places either in lakes, wells, spas or the sea.

There are many legends about Worms in the British Isles; one of the best known is the legend of the Lambton Worm. The Lambton Worm was caught by young Lambton when he was fishing in a stream. It was so small and ugly that he threw it contemptuously into a nearby well and returned home thinking no more about it. But the Worm did not remain in the well, as the legend states:-

> Meantime the Worm it grew and grew
> So lithlie and so strong,
> And stretched itself at morning prime
> An hundred yards along
> The river bank, and offtimes wrought
> Sad devastation wrong.

The Worm's appetite grew in proportion to its size; it became the scourge of the countryside, devouring sheep, lambs and calves and drinking the milk of a dozen cows at a single sitting. Young Lambton returned home from fighting in the Crusades and was horrified to see what had happened while he had been away. He was so determined to kill the monster that he went to an armourer and ordered an unusual suit of mail with the front and back studded with heavy steel blades. Wearing this curious armour, he went down to the river where he found the Worm, lapped nine times around a hill on the river bank, fast asleep. Lambton climbed on top of a rock in the middle of the river and blew his horn. The Worm awoke, uncoiled itself and slithered down to the river where the hero stood. It wound itself around the knight and tightened its folds in an effort to crush him, but the strong blades on the knight's armour carved into its flesh and soon the Worm was cut into little pieces, which fell into the river and were carried away with the current. If the pieces of the Worm had not been carried away immediately by the river, this reptile, like the Hydra, would have had the power to regenerate itself.

In the north of England there is a legend of a maiden who was changed into a 'Laidly Worm' until she was released by a kiss. Another, the Wode Worm of Linton, was killed by having a lump of peat dipped in burning pitch thrust down its throat. In the south, a woodman killed a 'Vurm' with his axe when he accidentally sat on its back thinking it was a log.

The Worm is a symbol of power deliberately put to an evil purpose. Jung defines it as a libidinous figure that destroys life. It denotes crawling, knotted energy without vivifying properties.

WYVERN

See also Dragon, Worm.

Definite changes began to happen to the shape of the Worm or Orm in Europe about the time that King Canute came to the throne of England after the Danish invasions. Before this, the Worm was represented in carvings and illustrations as a large horned serpent, but now it was portrayed as a much more ornate creature with bat-like wings, a fierce looking head and two legs. It became known as a Wyvern, a word which comes from the French word 'wivere' meaning both viper and life. The lifegiving aspect of the Wyvern's name makes it consanguineous with the powers of the dragon when it appeared in a non-Christian context representing the vital energies of water. However, the lifegiving aspects of the Wyvern often seem to be inverted for the Wyvern that appears in some of the folklore of Europe is a vicious and fierce predator, taking instead of giving life. In heraldry it is the symbol of war and pestilence.

A Wyvern has its jaws split open. The letter H from a 16th century AD manuscript.

An illustration of the folk tale of the 'Wyvern of Cynwch Lake'.

A Yale from the 12th century Roxburgh Bestiary.

YALE

The Yale, which is also known as the Eale and the Jall can be found in bestiaries and in heraldry. It is described as being as big as a horse, goat-like – 'Ya- el' means mountain goat in Hebrew – with teeth like a boar, the feet of a Unicorn, spots of various colours and a self-satisfied expression. The Yale is reputed to be able to adjust its outlandishly long horns, folding one back when it is fighting so as to have one sharp weapon ready when needed. Animals very like this description were portrayed in Indian art as guardians against evil spirits.

The Yale was described by Pliny the Elder, who said that it was the size of a hippopotamus with the jaws of a boar, an elephant's tail, movable horns and was coloured black or tawny.

In the heraldry of England it is one of Queen Elizabeth II's beasts. These are a set of carved animals that illustrate, with heraldic emblems, the Queen's royal ancestry. The Yale that is depicted here is the Yale of Beaufort and represents the House of Lancaster.

ZIPHIUS

In bestiaries the Ziphius or water owl was described as a fish of monstrous size with an owl's head, horrible eyes, a beak that was wedge-shaped and a mouth as huge as a pit. It was greatly feared by the seamen of northern waters as it would attack every ship it came across. It has no connection with the whale of the modern genus Ziphius or with the Greek swordfish Xiphias.

ZÛ

See also Imdugud, Human-headed birds

Zû is the stormbird or bird-centaur that is the chief protagonist in a myth which has an identifiable pictorial representation on some Mesopotamian clay tablets that were made after 3500 BC when the Sumerians first settled in the area. Unfortunately, some of the tablets are not in very good condition, making parts of the story rather fragmentary. The complete myth has had to be built up from a number of different manuscripts with some variation in detail.

A bird-like figure on some cylinder seals has been identified by Henri Frankfort as Zû who is portrayed with the body of a bird and a bearded, human head and arms. He may be a lesser deity but is always in conflict with the chief Gods. In a myth that parallels the Babylonian creation mythology of the dragoness Tiāmat, Zû stole the Tablets of Destiny from the high God Enlil while he was washing, and flew away with them to his home in the mountains. One of the Gods (the tablet on which this part of the story is recorded is too damaged to say exactly who the challenger was, but Ninurta is mentioned later in the manuscripts) undertook the task of pursuing Zû and bringing back the sacred artifacts. Zû was vanquished and killed and the Gods regained possession of the tablets.

It is thought that in the older Sumerian mythology the emblem of the god Ninurta-Ningirsu – the lion-headed eagle Imdugud – was probably a precursor, in a different form, of Zû. In Akkadian mythology Imdugud's powers are transferred to Ningirsu of Ladash's defeated enemy Zû.

The Yale, one of the sculptures of the King's Beasts at Hampton Court Palace, England.

Below:
A Water Owle. Detail of one of the Oxburgh hangings, 1570.

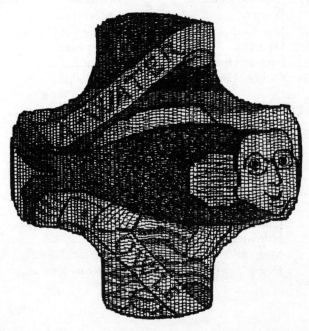

Index of Alternative Names

Drakon	Dragon
Eale	Yale
Earth Monster	Feathered Serpent
Ech-ushkya	Hippocamp
Echeneis	Remora
Empusae	Lamia
Endrop	Hippocamp
Ercinee	Luminous Birds
Erechtheus	Cecrops
Eurale	Gorgon
Fafnir	Dragon
Fastitocalon	Aspidochelone
Faun	Satyr
Fenriswulf	Ferir
Fish-goose	Falcon-fish
Fox-spirit	Fox
Fox-fish	Falcon-fish
Fu-ts'ang	Oriental Dragon
Furies	Erinneys
Gabriel Rachet Hounds	Dog
Gargouille	Gargoyle
Garm	Cerberus
Genius	Serpent
Girtablulu	Scorpion Man
Goat Fish	Capricornus
Goblin Fox	Fox
Goborchinu	Hippocamp
Gorgos	Gorgon
Great Fish Of The Abyss	Leviathan
Green Lion	Lion
Griffin	Griffon
Gryphon	Griffon
Gudanna	Bull
Guivre	Horned Serpent
Gullinbursti	Goldbristles
Gulo The Glutton	Gulon
Gwagwakh-walanooksiway	Cannibal Birds
Hai Ho Shang	Merman
Haietlik	Lightning Monster
Halibut	Thunderbird
Harmachis	Sphinx
Hävfine	Mermaid
Hea Bani	Centaur
Hieracosphinx	Sphinx
Hildisuin	Goldbristles
Ho-o	Fêng Huang
Hokhiku	Cannibal Birds
Hordeshyrde	Dragon
Hounds Of Hell	Dog
Hounds Of Heaven	Dog
Hrimfaxi	Horses Of The Sun
Huginn	Raven
Ichthyocentaur	Centaur
Ipopodes	Centaur
Irish Hounds	Dog
Jall	Yale
Jeduah	Lamb
Jenny Greenteeth	Nixies
Jerff	Gulon
Jinshin Uwo	Eel
Jormungand's Worm	Midgard's Worm
Ka-en-ankh Nereru	Sepent
Karkadann	Unicorn
Kelpie	Hippocamp
Kerkes	Phoenix
Ki-lin	Ch'i-lin
King Pratie	Bunyip
Kinnara	Human Headed Bird
Kirin	Ch'i-lin
Krake	Kraken
Kraxe	Kraken
Kreutzet	Roc
Kukulcan	Feathered Serpent
Kurdan	Bull
La Velue	Pedula
Ladon	Dragon
Lahamu	Tiāmat
Leopard	Panther
Leucrocuta	Leucrota
Licorn	Unicorn
Lilith	Dracontopides
Lion Dog	Dog
Lion Griffon	Griffon
Lotan	Leviathan
Loup Garou	Werewolf
Lucidius	Luminous Birds
Lucina	Luminous Birds
Lumerpa	Luminous Birds
Luna Hare	Hare
Lung Wang	Oriental Dragon
Lung	Oriental Dragon
Manabozho	Hare
Manabush	Hare
Manticora	Manticore
Mantiserra	Manticore

Maremaid.........................Mermaid
Mari...............................Aitvaras
Martikhora.......................Manticore
Medusa...........................Gorgon
Melusina..........................Melusine
Merdu............................Mermaid
Merwer...........................Bull
Merrymaid.......................Mermaid
Milse ....Mermaid
Mimicke Dog....................Dog
Mnevis............................Bull
Monk Fish........................Merman
Monkey ....Hanuman
Moon Rabbit.....................Hare
Muninn...........................Raven
Murghi-i-adami ....Human Headed Bird
Nemean Lion....................Lion
Nereid............................Mermaid
Nessus ....Centaur
Nidhogg ....Midgard's Worm
Ning-yo ....Mermaid
Nix................................Nixies
Nu Kua ....Fu-Hsi
Nycticorox ....Pelican in her Piety
Oannes............................Capricornus
Oannes............................Merman
Ocypete ....Harpy
Old Man of
   the Sea ....Merman
One Horned Bull..............Bull
Onocentaur......................Centaur
Onyx Monoceros ....Unicorn
Ophion ....Serpent
Orm..............................Worm
Ounce ....Panther
Ouroboros........................Serpent
Padfoot ....Dog
Panthera ....Panther
Papstesel..........................Ass
Pard...............................Panther
Pardalis...........................Panther
Pardel.............................Panther
Pardus............................Panther
Peg Powler.......................Nixies
Podarge...........................Harpy
Poqhirāj..........................Pegasus
Proteus...........................Merman
Puk ....Dragon
Pyong ....Roc

Pyrallis ....Salamander
Python............................Serpent
Qiqion ....Dog
Quetzalcoatl.....................Feathered Serpent
Ram Fish.........................Capricornus
Ram-headed
   Serpent..........................Horned Serpent
Raven Genius....................Raven
Red Lion ....Lion
Rukh..............................Roc
Sachrimnir.......................Goldbristles
Safat...............................Dragon
Satyral ....Manticore
Schachi Hoko...................Hai Riyo
Scoffin ....Basilisk
Sea Hog...........................Hog Fish
Sea Horse.........................Hippocamp
Sedus ....Lamassu
Sesha ....Serpent
Seven Whistlers................Dog
Seven-eyed Lamb.............Lamb
Shaggy Beast.....................Pedula
Shen Lung ....Oriental Dragon
Shen Nung ....Fu Hsi
Shrike ....Dog
Simargl ....Senmurv
Simurg ....Senmurv
Simyr..............................Senmurv
Sinam ....Senmurv
Sirrush.............................Mushussu
Skinfaxi ....Horses Of The Sun
Skoll..............................Fenrir
Snake Griffon....................Griffon
Soul Bird ....Ba
Stheno ....Gorgon
Stomach Faces ....Gryllus
Strong Toad......................Toad
T'ien Kou ....Dog
T'ien Lung ....Oriental Dragon
Tarasque ....Dragon
Tarw Elgan.......................Bull
Tatsu...............................Oriental Dragon
Teumessian Vixen.............Fox
Thelxiepea ....Siren
Three-legged Ass ....Ass
Three-legged Toad...........Toad
Thu'ban...........................Dragon
T'ien Kou ....Dog
T'ien Lung ....Oriental Dragon

Ti-lung	Oriental Dragon	Werepanther	Werewolf
Tobi Tatsu	Hai Riyo	Weretiger	Werewolf
Triton	Merman	Whale	Aspidochelone
Tunatabah	Bunyip	Wild Hunt	Dog
Unicorn Fish	Falcon-fish	Winged Bull	Bull
Uraeus	Serpent	Wivre	Vouivre
Vegetable Lamb	Lamb	Wizard's Shackle	Eel
Vircolac	Werewolf	Wouivre	Vouivre
Vitra	Serpent	Wulungu	Rainbow Monster
Vivere	Wyvern	Yellow Dragon	Oriental Dragon
Vulkodlac	Werewolf	Yfrit	Griffon
Vurm	Worm	Ying Lung	Oriental Dragon
Water Horse	Hippocamp	Yülunggu	Rainbow Monster
Water Owl	Ziphius	Yü Lung	Oriental Dragon
Waukheon	Thunderbird	Zägh	Human Headed Bird
Werejaguar	Werewolf	Zaltys	Aitvaras
		Zaratan	Aspidochelone

Bibliography

ALEXANDER, H (trans). **Beowulf**. Penguin 1973

ALEXANDER, M. **British Folklore, Myths and Legends**.
George Weidenfeld & Nicholson Ltd. 1982

ALLEN, J,R,. **Early Christian Symbolism in Great Britain and Ireland**.
London 1887

ALLEN, J. &
  GRIFFITHS, J. **The Book of the Dragon**. Orbis 1979

ANTIQUARIES,
  Society of. **5th Series**. Newcastle 1954

APULEIUS. **The Golden Ass**. trans. R.Graves. Penguin 1950

ARCHAEOLOGICAL INSTITUTE
  JOURNAL. **LXV 311 (1909). LXIX 381 (1912)**

BARBER, R. &
  RICHES, A. **A Dictionary of Fabulous Beasts**. Boydell Press 1971

BARING GOULD, Rev.S. **Church Dedications**. London 1907

BARING GOULD, Rev.S. **Curious Myths of the Middle Ages**. London 1867

BARING GOULD, Rev.S. **The lives of British Saints**. London

BAYLEY, H. **The Lost Language of Symbolism**. William & Northgate 1912

BIBLE. **Various editions**

BINDER, P. **Magical Symbols of the World**. Hamlyn 1972

BORD, J. **Mazes & Labyrinths of the World**. Latimer 1976

BORDMAN, J. **Greek Art**. Thames & Hudson 1964

BORGES, J.L. **The Book of Imaginary Beings**. Jonathan Cape 1970

BRANSTON, B. **The Lost Gods of England**. Thames & Hudson 1957

BRIGGS, K. **Dictionary of British Folktales**. London 1971

BROWN,P.(selector). **The Book of Kells**. Thames & Hudson 1981

BUDGE, Sir E.A.T.W. **The Gods of the Egyptians**. Methuen 1904

BURLAND, C. **Myths of Life & Death**. Macmillan 1974

BURLAND, C. &
  FORMAN, W. **Feathered Serpent & Smoking Mirror**. Orbis 1975

CAMBELL, J. **The Mythic Image**. London 1974

CAMBRENSIS, G. **The Historical Works of Giraldus Cambrensis**.
trans. T.Forester, R.C.Hoare, Rev. T. White. London 1913

CAVE, C.J.P,. **Roof Bosses in Medieval Churches**. London 1948

CAVENDISH, R. (editor). **Mythology**. Orbis 1980

CAVENDISH, R. (editor). **Man Myth & Magic**. Purnell

CHARPENTIER, L. **The Mysteries of Chartres Cathedral**. R.I.L.K.O. 1983

CIRLOT, J.E. **A Dictionary of Symbols**. Routledge 1988

CLEBERT, J.P. **Bestiaire Fabuleux**. Editions Albin Michel. Paris 1971

COOK, R. **The Tree of Life**. Thames & Hudson 1974

COOPER, J.C. **An Illustrated Encyclopaedia of Traditional Symbols**.
Thames & Hudson 1978

COPPER, B. **The Werewolf**. St Martin's Press New York 1977

COSTELLO, P. **The Magic Zoo**. Sphere Books 1979

COTTRELL, L. **Lost Cities**. Pan 1961

CYR, D.L. (editor). **Exploring Rock Art**. Stonehenge Viewpoint. California 1989

DAMES, M.   **The Avebury Cycle**. Thames & Hudson 1977
DANCE, P.   **Animal Fakes and Frauds**. Sampson Low 1976
DE ROLA, S.K.   **Alchemy - the Secret Art**. Thames & Hudson 1973
DE SANTILLANA, G. &
  VON DECHEND, H.   **Hamlet's Mill**. Macmillan 1969
DE VISSER, M.W.   **The Dragon in China and Japan**. Amsterdam 1858
DE VRIES.   **Dictionary of Symbols**
DILLON, M. &
  CHADWICK, N.   **The Celtic Realms**. London 1967
DINSDALE, T.   **The Leviathans**. Futura 1966
DURHAM,M.   **The Dragon and the Vine**. Folklore 43 no.3. Folklore Society 1932
ELLIOT SMITH, G.   **The Evolution of the Dragon**. London 1919
FAULKNER, R.O.   **The Ancient Egyptian Book of the Dead**. Guild 1972
FERGUSON, J.   **Encyclopedia of Mysticism and the Mystery Religions**. Thames & Hudson 1976
FONTENROSE, J.   **Python**. University of California & Los Angeles
FOX-DAVIES, A.C.   **Complete Guide to Heraldry**. Nelson & Sons
FRANKFORT, H.   **Cylinder Seals**. Macmillan 1939
FRANKFORT, H.   **Kingship & the Gods**. University of Chicago Press 1948
FRAZER, J.G.   **The Golden Bough**. Macmillan 1957
GETTINGS, F.   **Encyclopaedia of the Occult**. Rider 1987
GETTINGS, F.   **Visions of the Occult**. Rider 1987
GESNER, C.   **Historia Animalium**. Frankfurt 1617
GIFFORD, D.   **Warriors, Gods & Spirits**. Peter Lowe 1983
GOULD, C.   **The Dragon**. Wildwood 1977
GOULD, C.   **Mythical Monsters**. Allen 1886
GRAVES, R.   **The White Goddess**. Faber & Faber 1961
GRAVES, R (trans.).   **The Greek Myths**. Penguin 1955
GRUENWEDEL, A.   **Buddhist Art in India**. London 1965
HALL, A.   **Monsters & Mythic Beasts**. Doubleday, New York 1967
HARGREAVES, J.   **The Dragon Hunter's Handbook**. Granada 1983
HARGREAVES, J.   **The Signs of the Zodiac**. Kedleston Press 1988
HARTHAN, J.   **Books of Hours and their Owners**. Thames & Hudson 1982
HARTHAM, J.P.   **Animals in Art. No 9 Medieval Bestiaries**. London 1949
HAWLEY, W.M.   **Oriental Culture Chart No 13**. 1946
HEER, F.   **The Medieval World**. London 1962
HINNELLS, J. R.   **Persian Mythology**. Hamlyn 1973
HOGARTH, P. &
  CLERY, V.   **Dragons**. Jonathan Jaines 1979
HOLLIDAY, F.W.   **The Dragon & the Disc**. Futura 1973
HOLM, B.   **Crooked Beak of Heaven**. University of Washington Press 1972
HOLT, J.   **Dragons**. Gothic Image 1978
HOOKE, S.H.   **Middle Eastern Mythology**. Penguin 1963
HOWEY, M.O.   **The Horse in Magic & Myth**. London 1923
HOWEY, M.O.   **The Encircled Serpent**. New York 1955
HUXLEY, F.   **The Dragon - Nature of Spirit - Spirit of Nature**. Thames & Hudson 1979
IONS, V.   **The World's Mythology**. Hamlyn 1978
IVES, S.A.   **An English 13th Century Bestiary**. London 1942

144

IVIMY, J.   **The Sphinx & the Megaliths**. Sphere 1976
JUNG, C.G.   **Alchemical Studies**. Bollingen Foundation New York 1967
KAUFFMANN, C.M.   **An Alterpiece of the Apocalypse**. Victoria & Albert Museum 1968
KENTON, W.   **Astrology - The Celestial Mirror**. Thames & Hudson 1974
KLINGENDER, F.D.   **Animals in Art & Thought**. 1971
KOSUGI, K.   **Nippon No Non Yo**. 1977
KRAMER, S.N.   **Cradle of Civilisation**. 1967
LAINEZ, M.M.   **The Wandering Unicorn**. Hogarth Press 1983
LAMY,L.   **Egyptian Mysteries**. Thames & Hudson 1981
LAYARD, J.   **The Lady of the Hare**. Faber & Faber
LAROUSSE.   **Encyclopaedia of Mythology**. 1962
LEACH, M.   **Funk & Wagnall - Standard dictionary of Folklore**. New York 1972
LEADER, E.   **The Great Hound of the Parrett River**. R.I.L.K.O. 1985
LE CLERC, G.   **A Bestiary of Guillaume Le Clerc**. Leipzig 1890
LLOYD-JONES, H.   **Mythical Beasts**. Duckworths 1980
LUM, B.P.   **Fabulous Beasts**. Thames & Hudson 1952
LURKER, M.   **The Gods & Symbols of Ancient Egypt**. Thames & Hudson 1984
MAC CANA, P.   **Celtic Mythology**. Feltham 1970
MACNAIR, P. HOOVER,
    A. NEARY, K.   **The Legacy**. British Columbia Museum 1980
MARKS, R. &
    MORGAN, N.   **The Golden Age of English Manuscript Painting**.
                                   Chatto & Windus 1981
MARRIOTT, A. &
    RACHLIN.   **American Indian Mythology**. New American Library 1968
MARTIN, B.W.   **Dictionary of the Occult**. Rider 1979
MATSUMOTO, S.   **Kirin**. 1932
MODE, H.   **Fabulous Beasts & Demons**. Phaidon 1973
NEUBECKER, O.   **Heraldry**. Macdonald & James, 1977
O'MORGAN,M.   **The Mabin of the Mabinogion**. R.I.L.K.O. 1983
ORR, R.   **Mammals of Britain & Europe**. Pelham 1983
OVID, M.M.Innes (trans).   **The Metamorphoses of Ovid**. Penguin 1955
PAGE, M.   **Encyclopaedia of Things That Never Were**. Dragon's World 1985
PARKER, D.& J.   **The Immortals**. Webb & Bowyer 1976
PARROT, A.   **Nineveh & Babylon**. 1961
PEARS ENCYCLOPAEDIA OF MYTHS
    AND LEGENDS.   **Northern Europe, Southern and Central Africa - Ancient, Near
                                   and Middle East, Ancient Greece and Rome**. Pelham 1977
PERRY, J.T.   **Dragons and Monsters beneath baptismal fonts**. Relinquary S311
PLINIUS SECUNDUS, C.   **Natural History**. Loeb Classical Library 1958
RAWSON, P &
    LEGEZA, L.   Tao. Thames & Hudson 1973
READERS DIGEST
    ASSOCIATION.   **Folklore, Myths and Legends of Britain**. New York 1977
RHYS, J.   **Early Britain - Celtic Britain**
ROBINSON, M.W.   **Fictitious Beasts**. London 1961
ROSS, A.   **Pagan Celtic Britain**. Routledge & Columbia 1967
ROXBURGHE CLUB
    (Publishers).   **A 13th Century Bestiary in Almwick Castle** 1958
                                   also **The Apocalypse** 1876

RUNDLE CLARK, R.T.   **Myth and Ritual in Ancient Egypt**. Thames & Hudson 1959
SCREETON, P.   **The Lambton Worm**. Zodiac House 1978
SCHWALLER DE LUBICZ, I.
                Her-bak Egyptian Initiate. Inner Traditions 1956
SHEPARD, O.   **The Lore of the Unicorn**. New York 1930.
SHERIDAN, R. &
  ROSS, A.   **Grotesques & Gargoyles**. David & Charles 1975
SIMPSON, J.   **British Dragons**. Batsford 1980
SMITH, G.H.   **The Evolution of the Dragon**. London 1919
STONE, M.   **The Paradise Papers**. Virago 1976
SUSSEX ARCHAEOLOGICAL SOCIETY.
                Sussex Notes & Quiries 1940
TATLOCK, J.S.P.   **Dragons of Wessex and Wales**. Speculum VIII 1933
THEOBALDUS.   **Theobaldi Pysiologus**. Mittellateinische Studen Vol 6 1972
THURLOW, G.   **Biblical Myths & Mysteries**. Octopus 1974
TIME LIFE BOOKS.   **The Enchanted World - Magical Beasts**. 1985
TOPSELL,E.   **The History of Foure-footed Beastes**. London 1607
VOGH,J.   **The Thirteenth Zodiac**. Granada 1977
WERNER, E.T.C.   **A Dictionary of Chinese Mythology**. Julian Press Inc. 1961
WHEATLEY, D.   **The Devil and All His Works**. Hutchinson

GOTHIC IMAGE PUBLICATIONS

We are a Glastonbury based imprint dedicated to publishing books and pamphlets which offer a new and radical approach to our perception of the world in which we live.

As ideas about the nature of life change, we aim to make available those new perspectives which clarify our understanding of ourselves and the Earth we share.

Leylines and Ecology: An Introduction
William Bloom & Marko Pogacnik £2.25
Devas, Fairies and Angels: A Modern Approach
William Bloom...£3.50
Glastonbury Maker of Myths
Frances Howard-Gordon £4.95
The Tor Maze
Geoffrey Ashe £2.25
Spiritual Dowsing
Sig Lonegren £5.50
Needles of Stone Revisited
Tom Graves £6.95
Meditation in a Changing World
William Bloom..£6.95
Dragons Their History and Symbolism
Janet Hoult £4.95
The Green Lady and The King of Shadows A Glastonbury Legend
Moyra Caldecott £4.95

These titles are available from

**Gothic Image Publications
7 High Street
Glastonbury
Somerset
BA6 9DP**

Add 20% for postage and packing. Add 40% for Air Mail to USA and Canada.

We also produce a mail order list of the best in alternative books...
... and we organise tours of Ancient Sites in Britain and Ireland.

Write to us for further information.

DATE DUE

HIGHSMITH 45-220